CARD DESIGN
rubber stamping with
colored pencils and watercolors

DAVE BRETHAUER

Card Design: Rubber Stamping with
Colored Pencils and Watercolors
© 2007 by Dave Brethauer

Martingale & Company®
20205 144th Ave. NE
Woodinville, WA 98072-8478
www.martingale-pub.com

Printed in China
12 11 10 09 08 07   8 7 6 5 4 3 2 1

**Library of Congress Cataloging-in-
Publication Data**

Library of Congress Control Number:
2007018483

ISBN: 978-1-56477-780-5

CREDITS

President & CEO: Tom Wierzbicki
Publisher: Jane Hamada
Editorial Director: Mary V. Green
Managing Editor: Tina Cook
Technical Editor: Dawn Anderson
Copy Editor: Melissa Bryan
Design Director: Stan Green
Assistant Design Director: Regina Girard
Cover & Text Designer: Shelly Garrison
Photographer: Brent Kane

mission statement
Dedicated to providing quality products
and service to inspire creativity.

CONTENTS

INTRODUCTION

It has been over 10 years since I first began making my own greeting cards. Fresh out of college with my degree (in mechanical engineering!), I walked into a stamp store for the first time and was astonished at the possibilities. I had always been interested in art and was excited to find a way to express it in such a personal way. I bought a few stamping supplies to make some birthday cards and I was hooked, my engineering career over before it even started.

I learned as I went, discovering all the little techniques that make a card beautiful, and the basics for creating a card that looks neat and professional—crisp folds, proper cutting, the right inks. I wanted to create little works of art for my friends and family, so I picked up ideas about color, how to paint, and how to use colored pencils. I switched from trying to put every stamp I owned onto one card to a more simple, composed style.

All of the ideas and techniques are pretty basic, but when you put them together, you can make someone really notice what you created for them.

So that's what this book is all about—sharing what I have learned with you. I have devoted two sections of this book to basics for colored-pencil and watercolor techniques. These sections are full of all the details you'll need to learn in order to make your greeting-card art really stand out. The section titled "Design Techniques" is a collection of ideas and projects to try once you are familiar with the basics. Specific instructions for all the cards shown can be found at the back of the book.

Over the years I have found that a classic, uncluttered style is a great look and also an easy way to learn these techniques. Practice the ideas in the book and make the cards your own. Once you've got the basics down, you'll take your handmade cards in a whole new direction.

Dave

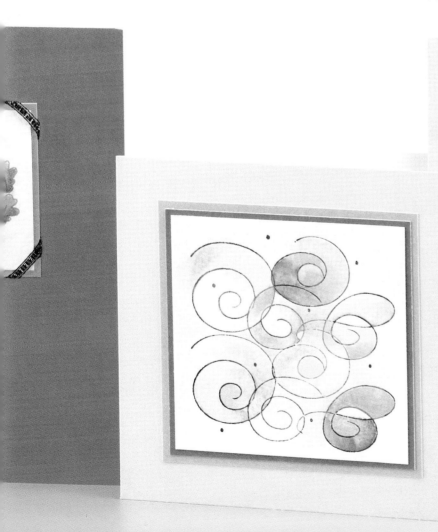

COLORED-PENCIL **basics**

Colored pencils are available in a huge array of colors and are capable of such flawless blending, people are often amazed to see the results and discover that colored pencils were used. Coloring with pencils is slower than using watercolor paints, but it affords greater control. There's no liquid moving where you don't want it to, which minimizes the guesswork. Convenient and maintenance free, a good pencil sharpener is all you'll need to get started.

Choose pencils that are made with soft, wax-based pigments designed to color in areas, rather than hard leads meant for drawing fine lines. The softer pencils provide smooth, opaque coverage, which means they can be used on colored papers as well as white backgrounds. Select a pencil sharpener that doesn't vibrate the pencil very much, so as not to break the lead inside the pencil.

COLORED-PENCIL FADING

1. Determine the area you want the fade to cover. Visualize the fade as a gradual, even shift of color across the area. Starting at the "dark" side, burnish (press hard) the color into the paper using up-and-down strokes. At the same time, slowly move the pencil to the right, gradually letting up on the pressure to lighten the color. Strive for a smooth, gradual lightening, with no abrupt changes in color.

2. As you near the end of the area, use the lightest touch yet. To end the fade, barely touch the pencil to the paper so only a hint of pigment is applied.

3. Evaluate the fade. To smooth out jumps in color, make small circle strokes (about ⅛" diameter) in areas that need darkening.

BLENDING

Blending results when two or more colors are mixed together to create a new color. Colors close to one another on the color wheel are considered analogous and blend easily into one another. They provide a tone-on-tone look that gives an elegant and coordinated feel. Complementary colors are opposite on the color wheel (green and red, for example). When used together, complementary colors create a high-contrast, graphic, and exciting look to a project.

1. Pick two analogous colors (colors that are adjacent on the color wheel), such as chartreuse and canary yellow. Use the canary yellow pencil to draw a 1" x ¼" box.

2. Working from left to right, begin coloring inside the box with the canary yellow pencil. Start with heavy saturation and gradually fade out the color until it disappears about ¼" from the right edge.

3. Begin coloring in the box with the chartreuse pencil. This time, start with heavy saturation on the right and gradually fade the color toward the left, until the chartreuse disappears ¼" from the left edge. You will overlap some of the yellow area.

4. If you did both fades correctly, you should have a solid yellow area, about ¼" wide, at the left edge and a solid chartreuse area, also ¼" wide, at the right edge. Leave these areas alone.

5. Using the canary yellow pencil, burnish the middle area from right to left, crushing the green and yellow pigments together.

BLENDING TWO SIMILAR SHADES

Learning to blend takes practice, and using two colors close to each other on the color wheel is a good place to begin. Use the darker color as a first layer and blend over it with a lighter color for a smooth look.

A DAY AT THE ZOO
blend top to bottom

BALLOON SURPRISE
repeat blended color schemes

A PEA IN THE POD
blend toward the center

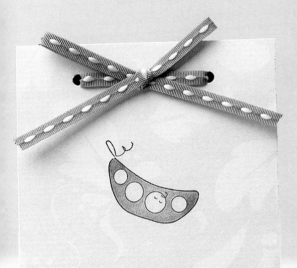

a pea in the pod

Have a Wonderful Birthday

POLKA-DOT PRESENT
blend two color schemes

SANTA CLAUS ORNAMENT
blending inward

DECK THE HALLS
add borders to a central image

HOLIDAY TOPIARY
add soft shading for depth

BLENDING THREE OR MORE SHADES

Once you've mastered layering and fading, you'll find you can blend an infinite number of colors. Make sure that you are fading evenly with each color and that you use firm pressure for the final blending.

EVENING SUNSET
add depth and light

PUMPKIN FULL OF TREATS
make parts of an image stand out

RAINBOW VASE
blend as many colors as you want

TIP Use the lightest common shade to blend over a group of colors. Different areas of a design may require different blending shades.

TIP Shading draws the eye to lighter areas in the design.

FROSTY SNOW SCENE
add interest by changing the direction of blending

TIP Placing bright colors next to dark areas of a design really makes the color stand out.

Alternatively, shade vertically, beginning with the lightest color at the horizon and ending with the darkest blue at the top.

ANALOGOUS COLOR SCHEMES

Analogous colors are colors that are next to each other on the color wheel, such as red and orange. For an analogous look, one might use red, orange, and all the reddish orange colors in between. Using similar colors or many shades of the same color can produce an elegant look. For more analogous color schemes, see the color wheel under "Blending" on page 7.

BIRTHDAY CAKE CELEBRATION
coordinate pencil colors with layered papers

SENDING YOUR BEST WISHES
use similar colors to create a clean look

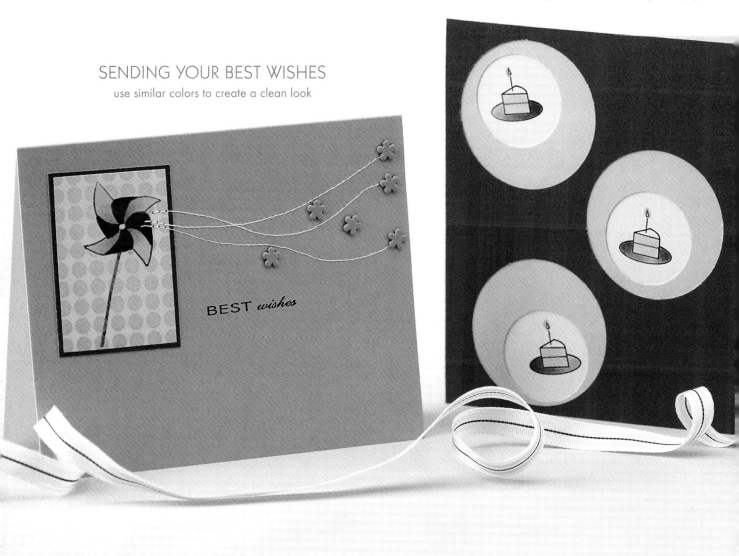

BEST *wishes*

SWIRLY BIRTHDAY CAKE
use a simple color scheme

HAPPY *birthday*

BUCKET OF BLOOMS
vary shades of the same color

ANALOGOUS COLOR SCHEMES

PUMPKIN PARTY
create shadows for added depth

||||| **TIP** ANCHORING THE IMAGE
||||| Add a shaded area below the stamped image to
||||| act as a shadow; this will help anchor the image.
||||| See the pumpkins at left.

THANK *you*

GIVING THANKS
stretching the color family: yellow + orange + pink

LEAFY GREETINGS
using a color scheme close to the
card color gives a tone-on-tone look

LEAFY GREETINGS
using bright analogous greens on a
warm yellow background makes
the leaf image pop

PILE OF PRESENTS

mix shaded and solid areas of similar colors

COMPLEMENTARY COLOR SCHEMES

When you want to make a part of an image stand out, use a color that contrasts against the rest of the color scheme. Complementary color schemes also tend to make a project look exciting and bright. For more complementary color schemes, see the color wheel under "Blending" on page 7.

under "Blending" on page 7.

THE BRIGHTEST HOUSE ON THE BLOCK
make a big, bold statement

A WRAPPED BOUQUET
a little contrast adds interest—pink and green are complementary

JOLLY OLD SAINT NICK
light and dark can make big contrast

THREE FUN STOCKINGS
complementary schemes add a whimsical feel

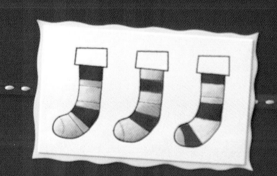

happy birthday

HAPPY BIRD-DAY

warm colors move forward while cool colors recede

FILIGREE BOUQUET

a neutral background of paper and ink can make a
complementary color scheme really stand out

FLOATING PETALS

pair complementary colors together for a cheery card

USING COLOR AS PATTERN

Adding pattern creates visual interest on even the simplest of images. Try using dots, stripes, and plaids in either complementary or analogous colors to add an artistic touch to your projects. For more information about complementary and analogous color schemes, see the discussion of the color wheel under "Blending" on page 7.

BON VOYAGE
use a sharp-tipped pencil to create texture and pattern

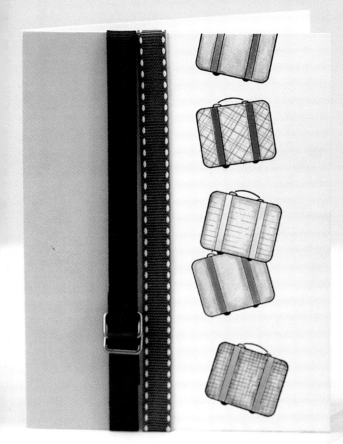

GIRLS' NIGHT OUT
leave areas uncolored to create dot patterns

TIP PREVENT BREAKING PENCIL LEAD
Soft lead breaks easily when sharpened to a point, so use light pressure when drawing line patterns.

PRISMATIC CHRISTMAS TREES
pattern concepts, such as rainbows, can make a big statement

HEARTFELT GREETINGS
use pattern to draw attention to a certain area

SNOWMAN AT SUNSET
creating a miniature image on shrink plastic
intensifies the colors

MINIATURE PEONY TILE
shading on a shrink-plastic image becomes
dramatic after shrinking

EXPERIMENTING WITH DIFFERENT SURFACES

Colored pencils can be used on a variety of surfaces and will behave a bit differently on each one. The soft lead of colored pencils works well on surfaces with a lot of "tooth," or texture. Colored pencils work wonderfully with the cushioned surface of watercolor paper, allowing the color to really build up thick layers as you work on it. Colored pencil takes very well to cardstock, allowing you to work on colored, plain, textured, and smooth papers. Glossy surfaces, such as shrink plastic, require some sanding before coloring to create some tooth.

A SIMPLE BOUQUET
watercolor paper provides a heavily
textured cushioned surface

For a different look, use the same colored-pencil scheme, but vary the card and watercolor paint colors. Notice the difference between the two cards. In the first card, the blue-on-blue scheme (an analogous color scheme) tends to recede and make the bouquet of yellowish orange flowers really "pop." In the pink-and-green combination, the pink really stands out against the green background (a complementary color scheme).

WATERCOLOR **basics**

There is nothing quite like the look of watercolor. A perfect wash of color across a sky or a smooth blend over a leaf can make a person look twice at your design. Watercolor techniques involve planning and timing but also stepping back and letting the paint do more or less its own thing. In this section, you will become familiar with the tools, materials, and techniques you will need to create beautiful watercolor designs.

BRUSHES

Paintbrushes are made either with synthetic fibers, such as nylon, or with natural fibers, such as animal hairs. Synthetic brushes are the less expensive of the two, and they do perform well, especially for small projects. Natural-fiber brushes lay paint down a little smoother and may last a bit longer.

Brush Shapes and Sizes

Paintbrushes are designed in different shapes for different jobs. Round brushes are the most effective for painting small, detailed areas. Flat brushes are more tailored for filling in large areas with a wash of color. As for size, keep in mind the area you will be painting when choosing the size of brush. I recommend a No. 4 or No. 6 round brush for painting in small images, such as those on a stamped greeting card. Use larger brushes, either round or flat depending on your preference, to fill in larger areas.

WATERCOLOR PAPER

Watercolor paper is a thick paper with a textured surface. The paint settles in the many dimples that cover the surface, producing a rich and intense color. Watercolor paper can be purchased in sheets, blocks, or tablets.

Watercolor Sheets, Blocks, and Tablets

Sheets of watercolor paper are available individually or in tablets and can be handmade or machine made. On small projects, curling tends to be minimal, but if you are painting a large area, tape the edges down to keep the work flat. A watercolor block is a stack of watercolor papers glued together on all four sides. You stamp and paint on the top sheet while it is still attached. The paint will not leak through to the next sheet, and the glued sides keep the paper flat so that you don't need to worry about curling as

you add water to the surface. When your finished work is dry, peel the top sheet off and trim it to size.

Paper Weights and Surfaces

I use 140 lb. paper, a common machine-made paper weight, for most of my projects. It is meant to soak up liquid without too much warping. Paper surfaces come in a variety of forms, but basically you will find either smooth (manufactured using a hot-press method) or rough (made with a cold-press method). Smooth surfaces stamp well but the paint tends to sink in quickly, requiring a quick hand with the watercolor. Rough surfaces float the color better, allowing for better movement of the paint, but the rough surface doesn't always stamp well. As you become more experienced, you will be able to use either surface well—it just takes practice.

Washes

A wash—the technique most often associated with watercolor—is a perfect, flowing gradation of color across an area. A wash may involve only one color that fades from dark to light, or it may feature a combination of colors, such as green flowing to blue flowing to purple.

Follow these instructions to create a wash.

1. Prewet an area with plain water. The surface should be slightly wet, so that you can see a sheen. If the area soaks up the water and dries quickly, add another layer of water.

2. Load a brush with paint and touch it to a corner of the prewetted area.

Observe the paint spreading into the wet area on its own.

3. Slowly brush the paint across the prewetted area, keeping the tip of the brush on the paper as much as possible. To avoid dried paint lines, work the brush along the edge of wet paint.

4. When your brush runs out of paint, pull it to the edge of the wet area and lift it off the paper. (Removing the brush in the middle will create a noticeable drop of color at that spot.) Reload the brush with paint and continue, starting inside the painted area and working toward your endpoint.

5. A successful wash will show a gradual change of color across the area. The color may fade out or randomly brighten and soften.

BLENDING WATERCOLOR PENCILS

Working with pencils is very easy because you can establish where colors will blend before you even add water.

PINWHEEL POSY
place color in the image where you want it
before painting with a wet brush

*colored sample before
blending with a wet brush*

BLENDING WATERCOLOR PAINTS

The advantage of paints is in their fluid nature, as they are designed to flow together and blend easily.

THREE TREES IN A ROW

prewet the area you will be painting before adding colors

BRUSH CARE Avoid letting your brushes stand in a cup of water for extended periods of time. When you finish painting, rinse your brush in clear water, pull the bristles to a point, and lay the brush flat to dry. Stand dry brushes upright in a container so the bristles aren't pressing against anything.

sample with two colors of paint before blending

BLENDING WATERCOLOR MARKERS

Water-based markers can be used like paints or pencils. When using them like a paint, create a palette on paper and lift ink off with a damp brush to apply to an image. When using them as a pencil, add ink to the specific area inside an image and pull the ink around with a damp brush.

VIVID VASES

similar to using watercolor pencils, add areas of ink beforehand and then blend with a wet brush

color application before blending

COLORING WITH WATERCOLOR PENCILS ON DRY PAPER

Watercolor pencils afford a great deal of control over where color is going to end up. Apply more pressure to the pencil for stronger color when shading, or less pressure for a softer, more pastel look. The pigment of the pencil dissolves by soaking up the water from the brush, so be sure to apply enough water to achieve a smooth look. The more water added to the colored area, the more blended it becomes.

HARVEST WREATH
pencils give you lots of control in small spaces

ORIENTAL POPPY
take your time getting the color where
you want it before you add water

...mple before
...ter is added

water blends the
colors together

TEA TIME
vary pencil pressure to create stronger
and weaker areas of color

FRUITS OF LABOR
lots of pigment and a small amount of
water yields brilliant color

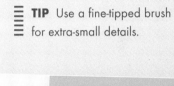 **TIP** Use a fine-tipped brush
for extra-small details.

A GIFT FOR YOU
oose between wetting the colored pencils
and leaving parts dry for sharp details

ALL BUNDLED UP
for "barely there" shading, use paint left
over on the brush from coloring other areas
of an image

WORKING DIRECTLY FROM THE PENCIL

For strong, smooth color in small areas, use a wet brush to pull paint directly from the tip of the pencil. The color is thick and relatively opaque when applied in this manner and works especially well for smaller areas.

DANCING BUTTERFLIES
a thick layer of color over the butterfly wings lends a soft, chalky appearance to the image

WEDDING CONGRATULATIONS
color fades out naturally as it is pulled across an image

TIP Painting directly from the pencil makes the color thick when applied. This can soften the hatched pattern on the wings.

BERRY BRANCHES
a halo of color around an image stamped in
black brightens an otherwise dark look

a new nest

A NEW NEST
a few quick splashes of color complete the
look of this change-of-address card

USING WATERCOLOR PAINTS FROM A PALETTE

Filling in large areas is a breeze when working with paints from a palette. Color is applied with little effort onto the paper and continues to mix together while settling into the surface. If the paper is wet, the paint will do most of the work for you by continuing to move even after you've finished with your brush. The excitement is in watching the results develop before your eyes.

WINTER TREE AT SUNSET
analogous colors and subtle shading fill the background with simple details

SPRING TREE
texture develops when the surface of the paper is dry

GAUGING INTENSITY
The colors in a wash lighten as they dry. If your wash looks a little stronger or darker when wet than you intended, then you're doing it correctly.

MODERN TREES
a simple wash technique makes beautiful backgrounds

EMBOSSED RESIST DAISIES
a simple resist technique will completely change the look of an image

APPLYING WATERCOLOR PAINTS DIRECTLY TO STAMPS

Brushing paint directly onto the stamp brings rubber stamping to a whole new level. When applying paint to the rubber (solid images work better than outline images), use a thick mixture of paint rather than a thin, watery mix. Add light colors first, and then dab on deeper colors here and there and allow the paints to blend a bit before stamping.

FALLING LEAVES
mixing color on the rubber creates
a painted-by-hand look

HARVEST LEAF
add water after an image has been
stamped to enhance areas of color

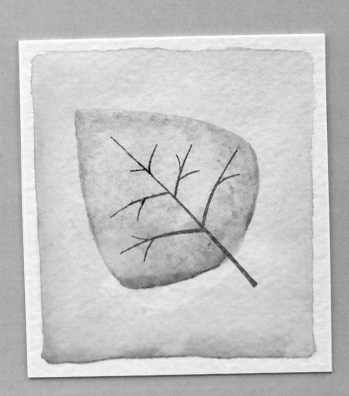

feel better soon

FEEL BETTER SOON
bigger images allow you to use a
wider color palette

USING WATER-BASED INK AS A PALETTE

Whether you use markers or inkpads, the techniques are the same here for achieving a watercolor look. You can make small patches of color with markers onto a scratch sheet of watercolor paper for a palette, or you can pull ink directly from an inkpad with a damp brush. Once you have loaded the brush, paint just as you would if pulling pigment from a palette of watercolor paints.

THANK YOU BOUQUET
for a stronger color and quick technique, add color to a stamped image as you would with watercolor pencils and then pull the color around with a wet brush

ROSE INVITATION
slowly build the color in layers to achieve a shaded look

FLOATING BLOOMS
mix colors as you layer them

APPLYING WATER-BASED INK DIRECTLY TO STAMPS

Use a few easy tricks to change a plain stamped image into watercolor artwork. Whether color is blended on the stamp or on the paper, the image is transformed into a unique piece of art.

OLD-FASHIONED ROSES
markers allow you to precisely place color on the stamp before blending

FIERY FLOWER
mix stamped colors with coordinating backgrounds

This is the image stamped for the first time after coloring. Notice how strong the color is. The same image was stamped a second time without reinking to make the card. Notice how much the image has softened while still retaining detail and even subtle color variations.

TIP Use a wet paintbrush to further blend colors on the paper after an image is stamped.

GENTLY FALLING PETALS
leave open spaces on the stamp for a faded look

WORKING WITH WATERCOLOR
TECHNIQUES ON CARDSTOCK

The main idea here is to limit the amount of liquid you put onto cardstock, because cardstock doesn't handle moisture very well. Stick with images that don't require a lot of coloring, or limit your use of watercolor techniques to specific parts of the greeting card.

BOXED PRESENTS
blend with less water on cardstock

JUST MARRIED
create shaded areas with watercolor pencils before applying water

THANK YOU, THANK YOU VERY MUCH
working from the tip of a watercolor pencil adds
only a tiny amount of water to the paper

WORKING WITH WATERCOLOR
TECHNIQUES ON WATERCOLOR PAPER

Watercolor paper is designed for watercolor techniques, so this is the easiest surface to work on. You can apply lots of water to blend, layer, and mix without worrying about oversaturating the paper. The texture of watercolor paper (hot press, which is smooth, or cold press, which is bumpy) creates a sophisticated feel on a greeting card.

SWIRLING RAINBOWS
work in steps so that areas don't blend together accidentally

KEEP ME IN STITCHES
hot press watercolor paper demands lots of water or the paint settles too quickly

THINKING OF YOU

line the inside of a greeting card
with a watercolor border

GARDEN OF FLOWERS

leave white space so that the
paper texture really shows

TIP Stamp an image in brown
to create a softer outline.

PEONY IN BLOOM

images with many fine details stamp
beautifully on smooth watercolor paper

design TECHNIQUES

Combining watercolor and colored-pencil techniques into the design of your cards is so gratifying. Once you have become comfortable with the basics of these mediums, you can put your new skills to use on all of your projects. In this section, watercolors and colored pencils are combined with other techniques to take handmade greetings up a notch. The final step is to assemble images into an aesthetically pleasing composition. I've always found that "simple is best," which may mean keeping images to a minimum or unifying a design with color. Find some inspiration here and remember to enjoy the process.

COMPOSITION

The look of your greeting is defined by how much or how little you put on your card. If there is a lot going on in the card layout, a central color scheme may keep things focused. If the mood of the card is more serene, a single image decorated in similar hues creates an elegant touch.

VINTAGE LOVE NOTE
tone down a busy image by using a tone-on-tone color scheme

GERBER DAISIES
cut-paper shapes create
depth and dimension

SNOWY GLOBE
leaving a portion of an image uncolored
creates a bright focal point

TIP Use embellishments that coordinate with your
stamped design—for example, fabric leaves that
echo the leaf motif on the base of this snow globe.

KNIT AND PURL

repeat elements of a stamped image, such as the
weave of the basket, in the design of the card

AUTUMNAL DRESS

echo the wavy shape of the leaves
with ribbon embellishment

CHERRY BLOSSOMS
build a scene using proportional designs

A TINY PART OF
SOMETHING BIGGER
use a strong, complementary color
to make an image stand out

TIP A warm color, such as red,
stands out against cool greens.

ZEN GARDEN
balance a neutral color scheme in greens
with a few complementary red accents

SKETCHED BRANCHES
incorporate broad pencil strokes into the design

PATTERN AND COLOR

Experimenting with the elements of pattern and color is the most artistically satisfy-
ing part of the process. You can make simple patterns by merely repeating an image
or color scheme in the design, or fill a space with brilliant details to create a more
complex pattern. Color can call attention to specific features of the card, or it can
affect the whole mood of your project.

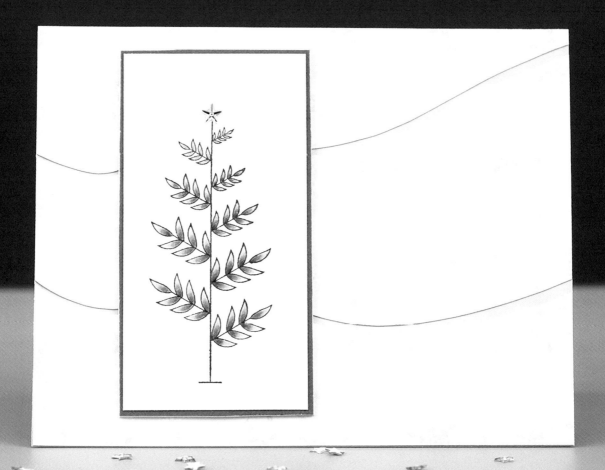

SNOWY WINTER TREE
shades of analogous blue pencils and
papers create a serene setting

BLOOMING POT OF TULIPS
vibrant color schemes are visually exciting

PUT YOUR LOVE ON THE LINE

repeat an image in coordinating colors for a simple effect

EASTER CHICK

delicate pastel shades layer
easily with one another

happy easter to you

FLORAL PRINT INVITATION

bold color makes a statement against a
neutral green-and-white color scheme

STRING OF HEARTS
coordinate broad color schemes
with similar layers of color

WATERCOLOR BACKGROUNDS

Designing over a customized watercolor background ensures that you can coordinate with the colors you plan to use in your design. Watercolor can provide a soft border that enhances the image or a bright backdrop for strong, graphic designs.

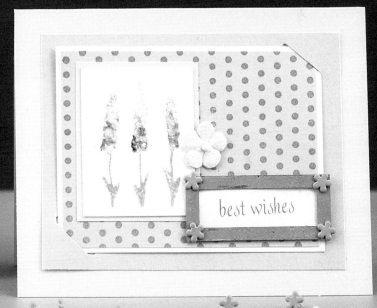

LATE FALL EVENING
blend several shades over an embossed image

POLKA-DOT FLOWER CARD
frame an image in soft color to create a glow

CARVED ACORNS
simple strokes of color enliven the
background behind a bold image

FLOATING FLOWER STEMS
markers dissolve easily into a
blended background

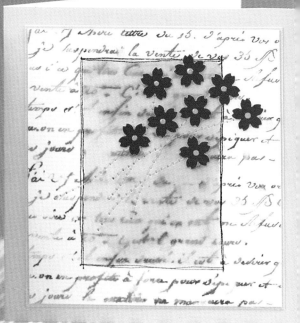

HEARTFELT TAG
a simple one-color wash over an embossed image
coordinates with a monochromatic color scheme

TEXTURE

Adding some visual interest to a card design can be achieved in many ways. Embellishments might include ribbon or thread, paper finishes, metal, patterned paper, contrasting colors—the list goes on and on. Strike a balance between chaos and a well-designed composition by choosing a focused color scheme.

STITCHED HEART
torn paper provides a nice contrast against a softly shaded background

BIRTHDAY BOUQUET
a metal frame is an eye-catching element over a tone-on-tone background

TIP Don't be afraid to color outside the lines; blurring around an image is a great watercolor look.

TULIP VASE
punch a subtle border around an
image with a sewing machine

PUMPKIN HARVEST
pick colors of ribbon and paint to coordinate
with the colors found in patterned paper

HALLOWEEN PARTY TAG
add some texture by sanding the
color off the edges of the paper

you are invited to a spooky Halloween Party

SPONGING

Sponging is a wonderful complement to delicate watercolor and colored pencil looks. Ink your sponge or dauber with pigment ink, which yields a softer, more painted look. Rub the sponge or dauber in circles a few times on a scratch sheet of paper to even out the color. Apply the sponge or dauber to the paper in a swirling motion, keeping the sponge on the paper without lifting. This technique builds up color slowly and yields the very best results.

ROW OF MISTY FLOWERS
use the sponging technique behind
an image to add a blur of color

SPONGING

FLOWER PATCH
match the sponged color to
a key color in the design

BLOOMING POINSETTIA
building up the ink slowly creates
a perfect halo of color

TIP Cutting the paper into a
wavy shape adds movement.

SNOWMAN IN A
CHRISTMAS SCARF
just a touch of color around the border
brightens the whole image

LACY OUTLINE FLOWERS
sponged areas blend beautifully as ink
colors are worked into each other

TRANSPARENT SURFACES

Working with sheer or transparent surfaces adds another creative factor to a card's overall design. Images stamped onto these surfaces seem to float, suspended above the paper beneath them. Use this to build a three-dimensional feel into your design.

CONFETTI SHAKER
a transparent layer creates a miniature shaker card

OVER THE MOON
color the back side of sheer vellum to eliminate the look of stroke marks

A HANDFUL OF LUPINES
a flower print is stamped on a transparency and
then repeated on the card below for a layered look

THREE VASES
a swirly watercolor background is
a great backdrop for a simple outlined image

TIP Include a plain card in which
to write your greeting when send-
ing a transparency project like this.

CHALKING

The method of applying chalk powder to an image on paper is a stunning technique. It mimics the look of watercolor but has a lighter, more ethereal feel to it. The stamped images blur a little as they are filled in with chalk dust, changing from one shade to the next seamlessly. Chalking is a great way to make your projects take a more serious and subdued tone.

SHOWER

PARTY LANTERNS
a blur of subtle color picks up
all the details of a stamped image

Please join us for Erin's Birthday party on August 24 at 6 pm

CONTEMPORARY
SHOWER INVITATION
a bold image floats over the muted
shades of a background pattern

A GOOD FRIEND
large images show how well
chalks blend together

THANKS FOR YOUR FRIENDSHIP
a fine-tipped brush adds light and
dark details to an image

TIP When applying chalk, hold the brush
at a very shallow angle and brush gently,
so that the inked image gets chalk but the
surrounding paper receives hardly any.

MATERIALS AND **instructions**

Page 8   A Day at the Zoo
MATERIALS

Stamps: Memory Box—B630 Lion, B623 Croc, and C631 Giraffe

Patterned paper: Memory Box—Homespun Collection

Cardstock: Memory Box—Sweet Corn

Note card: Memory Box—Eggshell

Colored pencils: Prismacolor—1034 Goldenrod, 914 Cream, 911 Olive Green, and 1005 Limepeel

Ink: Tsukineko—VersaFine Onyx Black

HOW TO:

Stamp the lion, croc, and giraffe with black ink onto the Eggshell note card. For the lion, add a first layer of Goldenrod at the bottom of the legs, softening as you move upward and fading out halfway up to the top of his body. Blend over the first layer with heavy pressure, using the Cream from the bottom of his body to the top. Color the mane with a solid layer of Goldenrod and then color the face with Cream. Color the giraffe in a similar manner. For the croc, begin with a layer of Olive Green at the feet and fade out as you move upward, ending about halfway up his body. Blend over the entire area with Limepeel, using heavy pressure. Trim the patterned paper and the Sweet Corn cardstock to size and mount to the card.

Page 8   Balloon Surprise
MATERIALS

Stamps: Memory Box—B284 Balloon and B291 Big Chick

Note card: Memory Box—Eggshell

Colored pencils: Prismacolor—1034 Goldenrod, 914 Cream, 926 Carmine Red, 1001 Salmon, 918 Orange, and 917 Sunburst Yellow

Ink: Tsukineko—VersaFine Onyx Black

HOW TO:

Stamp the chick and balloons with black ink onto the Eggshell note card. For the chick, begin with a Goldenrod base at the bottom, softening as you move upward. Blend over the chick with Cream using firm pressure. For half of the balloons, begin with Carmine Red at the base of a balloon, softening as you move upward, and fading out halfway up. Blend over the Carmine Red with Salmon, pressing hard over the entire balloon. For the other

half of the balloons, begin with Orange at the base, softening as you move upward, and fading out halfway up. Blend over the Orange with Sunburst Yellow, pressing hard over the entire balloon.

Page 9   A Pea in the Pod
MATERIALS

Stamps: Memory Box—B612 Pea Pod and B604 A Pea in the Pod

Patterned paper: Memory Box—6" x 6" Homespun Collection

Cardstock: Memory Box—Eggshell

Colored pencils: Prismacolor—911 Olive Green, 1005 Limepeel, and 989 Chartreuse

12" length of ⅛"-wide lime green ribbon

Ink: Tsukineko—VersaFine Onyx Black

⅛" hole punch

HOW TO:

Stamp the pea pod and "a pea in the pod" with black ink onto patterned paper. Add a first layer of Olive Green on the right and left sides of the pea pod, lightening the pressure as you move toward the center and avoiding the circular peas. Pressing hard with the pencil, color over the Olive Green with Limepeel, again avoiding the peas. Color in the peas with Chartreuse. Layer the patterned paper over the cardstock and trim them to the same width, but trim each layer to a different length. Punch three holes near the top of the layered papers. Thread the ribbon through the outside holes from the front and then thread both ends through the center hole to the front. Tie the ends in a bow.

Page 9   Polka-Dot Present
MATERIALS

Stamps: Memory Box—B501 Dotty Gift and A230 Star Flower; Impress—2076 Wonderful Birthday

Cardstock: White; Memory Box—Eggshell and Meadow

Note card: Rubber Soul—Maize

Colored pencils: Prismacolor—911 Olive Green, 1005 Limepeel, 1002 Yellowed Orange, and 917 Sunburst Yellow

Ink: Tsukineko—VersaFine Onyx Black and VersaMagic Tea Leaves; Impress—Fresh Ink Celery

Corner rounder punch tool

HOW TO:

Stamp the gift with black ink onto white cardstock and also onto Eggshell cardstock. Color the gift on white cardstock using Olive Green as a first layer in the lower-right corner, lightening the pressure as you go toward the upper-left corner. Pressing hard, color over the Olive Green with the Limepeel pencil. Color inside the circles with Yellowed Orange, beginning at the upper left and fading halfway across the circle. Color over the entire inside of the circle with Sunburst Yellow to blend. Stamp the star flower in the two shades of green ink, alternating the colors across the Eggshell cardstock. Cut the gift image out of the white cardstock. Line it up with the gift image on the Eggshell paper and adhere in place. Stamp the birthday message in black. Trim, layer, and mount the papers to the card.

Page 10   Santa Claus Ornament
MATERIALS

Stamps: Memory Box—D721 Big Santa and CS-107 Ornaments Set

Cardstock: Memory Box—Cranberry and Meadow

Patterned paper: Memory Box—6" x 6" Elegant Holiday Collection

White note card

Colored pencils: Prismacolor—937 Tuscan Red, 923 Scarlet Lake, and 1018 Pink Rose

Ink: Tsukineko—VersaFine Onyx Black

Sewing machine and silver thread

HOW TO:

Open the note card and sew a curved line of silver thread across the card, just under the fold line. Stamp the Santa and two ornaments with black ink onto the white note card, so that the tops touch the thread line. Add a layer of Tuscan Red to the left and right sides of the Santa, fading as you move toward the center. Add some Tuscan Red underneath his belly, shading as you move down his legs to create a shadow. Using Scarlet Lake, blend over the Tuscan Red and the rest of his suit, avoiding the cuffs, mittens, and his belt. Color his hat with a solid layer of Scarlet Lake. Add pink to his nose and face. Stamp the ornaments onto a patterned paper and two colors of cardstock. Cut out selected sections of the stamped images and mount over the stamped images on the card.

Page 10   Deck the Halls
MATERIALS
Stamps: Memory Box—B723 Bird and F733 Holly Border

White note card

Colored pencils: Prismacolor—937 Tuscan Red, 923 Scarlet Lake, 916 Canary Yellow, 911 Olive Green, and 989 Chartreuse

Ink: Tsukineko—VersaFine Onyx Black

HOW TO:
Stamp the bird and holly borders with black ink onto the note card. For the bird, begin with a Tuscan Red layer at the bottom, softening as you move upward and fading out halfway up. Using Scarlet Lake, blend over Tuscan Red, pressing hard. Color in the beak with Canary Yellow. For the holly, color all the berries Scarlet Lake. For the holly leaves, start with a layer of Olive Green at the base of each leaf, softening as you move across the leaf and fading out halfway across. Blend over the Olive Green with Chartreuse, pressing hard to blend. Color the smaller leaves Chartreuse.

Page 11
Holiday Topiary
MATERIALS
Stamps: Memory Box—D731 Boxed Topiary and B730 A Holiday of Lights

Cardstock: White; Memory Box—Peapod

Note card: Memory Box—Cranberry

Colored pencils: Prismacolor—911 Olive Green, 1005 Limepeel, 923 Scarlet Lake, 943 Burnt Ochre, and 1034 Goldenrod

Ink: Tsukineko—VersaFine Onyx Black

1/8" circle punch

5" length of 3/8"-wide olive green ribbon

HOW TO:
Stamp the topiary and "a holiday of lights" with black ink onto white cardstock. Stamp the topiary separately onto Peapod cardstock. On the topiary stamped on white cardstock, begin with a soft layer of Olive Green around the outer edges of the leaves and also around the balls on the tree. Add a layer of Limepeel over the Olive Green and throughout the leafy area. Color in the balls with Scarlet Lake,

leaving a small uncolored area to act as a reflection of light. For the tree trunk, begin with a heavy layer of Burnt Ochre on the right side of the trunk and branches, softening as you move left. Add a layer of Goldenrod over the Burnt Ochre, pressing hard on the left edges. Color the inside of the planter box with a soft layer of Goldenrod. On the Peapod cardstock, add shading to the right side of the planter box with Olive Green. Add shading to the front of the planter box inside the frame, using a soft layer of Olive Green followed by a soft layer of Limepeel.

Cut the planter box from the Peapod cardstock and mount onto the White cardstock, aligning the images. Trim, layer, and mount the White cardstock to the Peapod cardstock, and then trim. Punch holes for inserting the ribbon. Insert the ribbon and mount the card.

Page 12
Evening Sunset
MATERIALS
Stamp: Memory Box—D134 Treescape

Cardstock: White; Memory Box—Gourd

Note card: Memory Box—Mango

Colored pencils: Prismacolor—995 Mulberry, 924 Crimson Red, 923 Scarlet Lake, 918 Orange, 1002 Yellowed Orange, 907 Peacock Green, 913 Spring Green, 1005 Limepeel, 989 Chartreuse, 914 Cream, and 911 Olive Green

Ink: Tsukineko—VersaFine Onyx Black

HOW TO:
Stamp the treescape with black ink onto white cardstock. Begin with a layer of Mulberry in the upper corners of the sky. Color heavily at first, fading toward the center of the image. Add a layer of Crimson Red, beginning on top of the Mulberry at the corners (pressing hard), and fading out about 1/8" beyond the Mulberry. Next add Scarlet Lake, layering on top of the first two colors and fading out a little further into the center. As you fade, create the impression of an arc of color around the center of the horizon. Add a layer of Orange, beginning at the upper corners and fading to the center, this time reaching the center point. Blend over the sky with Yellowed Orange, avoiding the darkest area at the corners so that they do not lighten in color. Use heavy pressure for the final blend.

For the foreground, start with a layer of Peacock Green at the lower corners, fading

toward the center. Add a layer of Spring Green, beginning at the corners on top of the Peacock Green and fading a little further toward the center. Add a layer of Limepeel, beginning almost at the corners, leaving a little bit of the darker color untouched, and fading further in toward the center, leaving a little white space right around the horizon. Add a layer of Chartreuse, beginning almost at the corners and fading near the horizon but leaving a small amount of white space at the center of the image. Blend over the foreground with a heavy layer of Cream, avoiding the corners so that they stay dark, but pressing hard over the rest of the ground area.

For the trees, begin with a layer of Olive Green in the lower-right corner of each tree, fading as you move up and to the left. Blend over the Olive Green and the rest of the tree space with Chartreuse. Cut out the image and mount onto Gourd cardstock. Trim to size and mount to the card.

Page 12   Rainbow Vase
MATERIALS
Stamps: Memory Box—D204 Tall Vase and E422 Black Eyed Susan

Cardstock: Memory Box—Eggshell and Sweet Corn

Note card: Memory Box—Gourd

Colored pencils: Prismacolor—918 Orange, 917 Sunburst Yellow, 911 Olive Green, 989 Chartreuse, 995 Mulberry, 926 Carmine Red, 1018 Pink Rose, 934 Lavender, 1024 Blue Slate, 1087 Powder Blue, and 938 White

Ink: Tsukineko—VersaFine Onyx Black

HOW TO:
Stamp the vase onto Eggshell cardstock with black ink. Mask the vase and stamp the flower so that it appears to be inside the vase. For the flower, add a layer of Orange near the dark center and fade downward along the petals, fading out halfway down. Blend over the Orange and the rest of the petal with a heavy layer of Sunburst Yellow. For the leaves, begin with a layer of Olive Green, fading out halfway along each leaf. Add a layer of Chartreuse over the Olive Green and the rest of the leaf. For the vase, beginning with Mulberry, shade in the lower-left portion of the shape, fading along the side and toward the middle of the image about 1/2". Next begin shading with Carmine Red, about 1/2" above the Mulberry area, fading in all directions and softly overlapping the Mulberry area. Next begin shading with Orange, another 1/2" above the Carmine Red area, fading in all directions along the side of the vase and softly overlapping the Carmine Red area. Continue

this process, traveling around the perimeter of the vase and overlapping each color. Before the final blending, there should be strong color around the edges of the vase and softer color in the center. For the final blend, use a White pencil to blend over the areas in the middle, avoiding the strong colors along the edges. Trim, layer, and mount the papers to the card.

Page 12 Pumpkin Full of Treats
MATERIALS

Stamp: Memory Box—F712 Candy Pumpkin

Note card: Memory Box—Eggshell

Colored pencils: Prismacolor—1032 Pumpkin Orange, 918 Orange, 917 Sunburst Yellow, 943 Burnt Ochre, 934 Lavender, 929 Pink, 994 Process Red, 992 Light Aqua, 1025 Periwinkle, 903 True Blue, 916 Canary Yellow, 913 Spring Green, and 989 Chartreuse

Ink: Tsukineko—Brilliance Graphite Black

HOW TO:

Stamp the image onto the Eggshell note card with black ink. For the pumpkin face, begin with a layer of Pumpkin Orange around the edges of the image, fading ⅛" in toward the center. Add a layer of Orange, beginning at the edges and fading at the center of the face. Blend over the two oranges with a heavy layer of Sunburst Yellow. Color the handle solid with Burnt Ochre. Color the candies with the remaining colors, adding small blended areas and contrasting stripes.

Page 13 Frosty Snow Scene
MATERIALS

Stamp: Memory Box—D320 House on the Hill

White cardstock

Note card: Memory Box—Blue Poppy

Colored pencils: Prismacolor—1007 Imperial Violet, 902 Ultramarine Blue, 906 Copenhagen Blue, 904 Cerulean Blue, 1087 Powder Blue, 1024 Blue Slate, and 1023 Cloud Blue

Ink: Tsukineko—VersaFine Onyx Black

HOW TO:

Stamp the house scene onto white card-stock with black ink. Blend Imperial Violet, Ultramarine Blue, Copenhagen Blue, Cerulean Blue, and Powder Blue for the sky, starting with the deepest colors on the left and right sides of the image and blending toward the middle. Add shadows of Powder Blue along the left and bottom inside edges of the tree, to the ground below the tree, and along the outside

lower edges of the house. Color the door side of the house with Blue Slate and color the window side of the house with Cloud Blue. Cut out the stamped scene and mount to the card.

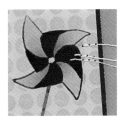

Page 14 Sending Your Best Wishes
MATERIALS

Stamps: Savvy Stamps—843G Large Graphic Dot Background, 648D Pinwheel, and 674B Best Wishes Sans Script

Cardstock: Memory Box—Cotton Candy and Currant

Note card: Memory Box—Sugar Plum

Colored pencils: Prismacolor—995 Mulberry, 994 Process Red, 993 Hot Pink, and 1018 Pink Rose

Ink: Tsukineko—VersaMagic Perfect Plumeria and VersaFine Onyx Black; Impress—Fresh Ink Sugar

Sewing machine and white thread

Mini flower brads

Needle tool

HOW TO:

Stamp the pinwheel with Perfect Plumeria onto Cotton Candy cardstock. Mask the pinwheel and stamp the dot background over the image with Sugar. On the dark part of the pinwheel flaps, add a layer of Mulberry on the outer edges, pressing hard and then fading as you get near the center. Add a blending layer of Process Red over the Mulberry all the way to the center, pressing hard. On the open area of the pinwheel flaps, add a layer of Hot Pink, beginning at the center and fading as you move toward the edges. Add a blending layer of Pink Rose over the Hot Pink all the way to the edge of the pinwheel, pressing hard. Trim, layer, and mount the papers to the card. Sew three wavy lines of thread from the pinwheel out to the right side of the card, suggesting the movement of wind. Poke holes in the card with the needle tool and install the flower brads.

Page 14 Birthday Cake Celebration
MATERIALS

Stamp: Memory Box—B292 Piece of Cake

Cardstock: Memory Box—Currant and Cherry Blossom

Note card: Memory Box—Cotton Candy

Colored pencils: Prismacolor—927 Light Peach, 916 Canary Yellow, 994 Process Red, and 993 Hot Pink

Ink: Tsukineko—VersaFine Onyx Black

1" and 2" circle punches

HOW TO:

Cut Currant and Cherry Blossom cardstock to match the card front. Punch 2" circles into the Currant cardstock three times. Layer the Currant cardstock over the Cherry Blossom cardstock and punch 1" circles into the Cherry Blossom through the previously punched holes, with the holes slightly off center. Glue the two papers together and mount onto the Cotton Candy note card. Stamp the cake onto the note card through the holes with black ink. Color the front of the cake with Light Peach and color the flame with Canary Yellow. Add a layer of Process Red to one side of the cake plate (you can vary this position on each plate) and fade to the middle. I used Process Red on both sides of the middle plate. Add a blending layer of Hot Pink by pressing hard over the plate area.

Page 15 Bucket of Blooms
MATERIALS

Stamps: Memory Box—B419 Flower Bucket; Impress—2046C Scallop Seal and 2048I Long Dot Star Border

Cardstock: Memory Box—Cherry Blossom

Note card: Memory Box—Cotton Candy

Colored pencils: Prismacolor—989 Chartreuse, 993 Hot Pink, 994 Process Red, and 1018 Pink Rose

Ink: Tsukineko—VersaFine Onyx Black and VersaColor Orchid and Opera Pink

HOW TO:

Stamp the flower bucket with black ink onto the Cotton Candy note card and also onto the Cherry Blossom cardstock. Stamp the scallop seal with Opera Pink around the bucket, over-lapping the base of the bucket image. Mask the seal and stamp the dot-and-star border with Orchid. Color the leaves and stems Chartreuse and color the inside of the bucket with a light layer of Hot Pink. Shade half of each flower with Process Red. Add a layer of Pink Rose over the Process Red and the rest of each flower to blend. Cut the bucket image out of the Cherry Blossom cardstock and glue over the stamped bucket on the note card.

Page 15 Swirly Birthday Cake
MATERIALS

Stamps: Savvy Stamps—435C Outline Swirl Cake and 672C Happy Birthday

Cardstock: Memory Box—Cotton Candy and Currant

Note card: Memory Box—Cherry Blossom

Colored pencils: Prismacolor—916 Canary Yellow, 918 Orange, 994 Process Red, 993 Hot Pink, and 1018 Pink Rose

Pink paper flower and pink brad

Ink: Tsukineko—VersaFine Onyx Black

HOW TO:
Stamp the cake onto Cotton Candy cardstock with black ink. Color the scallop trim and the glow of the candles with Canary Yellow. Color the base of the cake stand Orange. Blend the three shades of pink from left to right across the cake, starting with a layer of Process Red and fading as you get to the middle. Add a layer of Hot Pink, beginning on the left side and fading about three-quarters of the way across the cake. Add a final blending layer of Pink Rose, coloring hard over the entire area of the cake. Trim, layer, and mount the papers onto the card. Glue the flower to the card and install the brad. Stamp "happy birthday" in black.

Page 16 Pumpkin Party
MATERIALS
Stamp: Savvy Stamps—698F Pumpkin Trio

Patterned paper: Memory Box—6" x 6" Spooky Collection

Cardstock: Memory Box—Persimmon and Eggshell

Colored pencils: Prismacolor—1032 Pumpkin Orange, 918 Orange, 1002 Yellowed Orange, and 1034 Goldenrod

Ink: Tsukineko—VersaFine Onyx Black

HOW TO:
Stamp the pumpkins onto Eggshell cardstock with black ink. Shade at the bottom of the pumpkins, beginning with the darkest color, Pumpkin Orange. Fade the color halfway up. Add a little bit more Pumpkin Orange to the left and right sides of each pumpkin. Next add a layer of Orange on top of the Pumpkin Orange and fade a little further up the pumpkin and toward the center. Finish the pumpkins by blending over the entire area of each image with Yellowed Orange, pressing hard. Color the leaves on the tendrils with Goldenrod (making sure the pencil point is sharp so that you can easily stay inside the small space of each leaf). Next add a soft blur of Goldenrod underneath each pumpkin to create the idea of a shadow. For the shadow, a dull pencil works best so that stroke marks don't show. Trim the papers and mount the layers.

Violet Bouquet

Page 16 Giving Thanks
MATERIALS
Stamps: Savvy Stamps—673B Thank You Sans Script; Memory Box—E201

Cardstock: Memory Box—Eggshell and Mango

Note card: Memory Box—Sweet Corn

Colored pencils: Prismacolor—926 Carmine Red, 918 Orange, 916 Canary Yellow, 1001 Salmon, 1034 Goldenrod, and 943 Burnt Ochre

Ink: Tsukineko—VersaFine Onyx Black

HOW TO:
Stamp the bouquet onto Eggshell cardstock with black ink. Begin with a thin line of Carmine Red on the outer edge of each petal in the bouquet. Next add a layer of Orange, beginning on top of the Carmine Red and fading quickly to within 1/16" of the sides. Next, color the center of each flower with Canary Yellow, pressing hard. Add a layer of Salmon over the Carmine Red and Orange, fading up to but avoiding the center Canary Yellow area. Trace over the stems of the flowers with Goldenrod. Color the space between the flowers with a very soft layer of Burnt Ochre, and then add a soft layer of Salmon over the area. Trim, layer, and mount the papers to the card. Stamp "thank you" in black.

Page 17 Leafy Greetings in reds and oranges
MATERIALS
Stamps: Memory Box—C141 Large Oak Leaf and AA600 Tiny Oak Leaf

Note card: Memory Box—Sweet Corn

Colored pencils: Prismacolor—923 Scarlet Lake, 926 Carmine Red, 918 Orange, and 917 Sunburst Yellow

Ink: Tsukineko—VersaColor Marigold and VersaFine Onyx Black

HOW TO:
Stamp the large leaf with black ink onto the note card. Mask the large leaf and stamp the small leaf several times across the card with Marigold. Begin with a Scarlet Lake layer on the left and right sides of the large leaf, fading away just 1/4" from the sides of the leaf. Add a layer of Carmine Red over the Scarlet Lake and extend the fade 1/8" further toward the center. Add Orange over the Scarlet Lake and Carmine areas, fading toward the center and

leaving a small amount of uncolored area on either side of the centerline. Blend over the entire leaf with Sunburst Yellow, pressing hard.

Page 17 Leafy Greetings in greens
MATERIALS
Stamps: Memory Box—C141 Large Oak Leaf and AA600 Tiny Oak Leaf

Note card: Memory Box—Endive

Colored pencils: Prismacolor—911 Olive Green, 1005 Limepeel, and 989 Chartreuse

Ink: Tsukineko—VersaMagic Tea Leaves and VersaFine Onyx Black

HOW TO:
Stamp the large leaf onto the card with black ink. Mask the large leaf and stamp the small leaf several times across the card with Tea Leaves. Begin with an Olive Green layer along the right edge of the leaf and fade away just 1/4" from the edge. Add a layer of Limepeel over the Olive Green and extend the fade 1/8" further toward the center of the leaf. Add Limepeel to the left edge of the leaf as well, applying soft pressure. Blend over the entire leaf and on top of the Limepeel and Olive Green areas with Chartreuse, pressing hard.

Page 18 Pile of Presents
MATERIALS
Stamps: Impress—2075D Pinked Seal; Memory Box—C308 Pile of Gifts

Cardstock: White; Memory Box—Endive

Note card: Memory Box—Moss

Colored pencils: Prismacolor—911 Olive Green, 1005 Limepeel, 989 Chartreuse, and 916 Canary Yellow

Ink: Tsukineko—VersaMagic Key Lime and VersaFine Onyx Black; ColorBox—Moss Green

Corner rounder punch tool

5" length of 3/8"-wide lime green ribbon

Foam mounting squares

Sponge or sponge dauber

HOW TO:
Stamp the pile of gifts with black ink onto white cardstock. Mask the gifts and stamp the pinked seal over the image with Moss Green. Color five or six of the presents solid using any of the colored-pencil colors, trying not to use the same color for adjacent shapes. Shade the remaining presents, beginning with darker shades as the base colors and fading them out as you move across the area of each gift. Add a blending

layer on top of the first color, using a lighter shade and pressing hard over the entire area of the present. For the largest present draw lines across the box to create a pattern. Trim the papers to size and round the corners of the papers and note card. Wrap and secure the ribbon around the Endive cardstock and mount it to the note card with foam mounting squares. Sponge the edges around the stamped image with Key Lime and mount to the Endive layer.

Page 19 A Wrapped Bouquet
MATERIALS
Stamp: Memory Box—C416 Stem Bouquet

Cardstock: White; Memory Box—Endive and Granny Smith

Note card: Memory Box—Key Lime

Colored pencils: Prismacolor—911 Olive Green, 913 Spring Green, 989 Chartreuse, 1005 Limepeel, and 993 Hot Pink

Ink: Tsukineko—VersaFine Onyx Black

6" length of ⅛"-wide lime green satin ribbon

HOW TO:
Stamp the bouquet with black ink onto white cardstock and also onto Endive cardstock. On the white cardstock, color the wrapping-paper portion of the image, beginning with Olive Green at the right edge and concentrating the color at the upper-right corner and again at the lower-left edge. Fade the Olive Green toward the center on the right side and fade it upward on the left side. Add a layer of Spring Green over the first layer, extending the fade ¼" farther than the first layer. Add a final blending layer of Chartreuse, pressing hard over the whole wrap area. Set aside. On the Endive cardstock, add a soft layer of Limepeel over the stems that are tucked into the wrap. Using a sharp Chartreuse pencil, color the leaves on the stems, leaving five or six leaves uncolored at the tops of the stems. Use a sharp Hot Pink pencil to color in the remaining leaves. Cut the wrap out of the white cardstock and glue to the Endive cardstock, aligning over the stamped image. Trim, layer, and mount the papers to the card. Tie the ribbon into a bow and glue to the card.

Page 19 The Brightest House on the Block
MATERIALS
Stamp: Memory Box—E499 Lighted House

Cardstock: Memory Box—Endive

Note card: Memory Box—Granny Smith

Colored pencils: Prismacolor—937 Tuscan Red, 924 Crimson Red, 923 Scarlet Lake, 989 Chartreuse, 916 Canary Yellow, 1005 Limepeel, 911 Olive Green, and 918 Orange

Ink: Tsukineko—VersaFine Onyx Black

HOW TO:
Stamp the house onto Endive cardstock with black ink. Add a layer of Tuscan Red around the perimeter of the house, fading in about ⅛" toward the center. Next add a layer of Crimson Red around the perimeter of the house, overlapping the Tuscan Red and fading ⅛" beyond the first layer, toward the center of the house. Blend over the Tuscan Red, the Crimson Red, and the rest of house area with Scarlet Lake, avoiding the windows, doors, and lights. Color in the lights with Chartreuse, Canary Yellow, and Crimson Red. Color the roof with Limepeel. Add a layer of Olive Green for the door, beginning on the right side of the door and fading halfway across. Blend over the Olive Green with Chartreuse, pressing hard. For the windows, add a layer of Orange to the left or right side of each window, fading toward the center of the window. Blend over the Orange pencil with Canary Yellow. Trim the image and mount to the card.

Page 20 Jolly Old Saint Nick
MATERIALS
Stamp: Memory Box—E521 Jolly Santa

Cardstock: White

Note card: Memory Box—Endive

Colored pencils: Prismacolor—937 Tuscan Red, 924 Crimson Red, 916 Canary Yellow, 1024 Blue Slate, and 927 Light Peach

Ink: Tsukineko—VersaFine Onyx Black

White puffball

HOW TO:
Stamp the Santa with black ink onto the Endive note card and also onto white card-stock. On the Endive note card, color Santa's clothing by first adding a layer of Tuscan Red along the right and left edges of the suit top, and along the bottom of the suit pants and hat, fading out ¼" away. Add a layer of Crimson Red over the Tuscan Red, filling in the rest of the suit and hat, pressing hard to blend. Color the buckle Canary Yellow. On the white cardstock, add a soft line of Blue Slate along the left, right, and bottom edges of all the fur parts. Color the face Light Peach, leaving a white ring around the eyes. Cut out the fur parts, including the face, and glue onto the Endive note card. Adhere a puffball to the tip of the cap.

Page 20 Three Fun Stockings
MATERIALS
Stamp: Memory Box—D518 Christmas Stockings

Cardstock: White; Memory Box—Key Lime

Note card: Memory Box—Cranberry

Colored pencils: Prismacolor—911 Olive Green, 1005 Limepeel, 989 Chartreuse, 937 Tuscan Red, 924 Crimson Red, 923 Scarlet Lake, 1034 Goldenrod, and 916 Canary Yellow

Ink: Tsukineko—VersaFine Onyx Black

6½" length of ⅛"-wide red-and-white ribbon

HOW TO:
Stamp the stockings onto white cardstock with black ink. For stripes with a green color scheme, begin with Olive Green on one side and fade toward the center. Blend over with a layer of Limepeel. For a lighter blend of green, use Limepeel as a first layer and Chartreuse as a blending layer. For a red color scheme, begin with a layer of Tuscan Red and fade toward the center. Blend over the Tuscan Red with a layer of Crimson Red, pressing hard. For a brighter blend of reds, use Crimson Red as a first layer and Scarlet Lake as a blending layer. For yellow stripes, begin with Goldenrod and blend using a layer of Canary Yellow. Trim the image to size and mount onto the Key Lime cardstock. Using plain scissors, cut a freehand wavy edge close to the edge of the white cardstock to create a Key Lime border. Glue ribbon to the Cranberry note card and mount the stockings image over the ribbon.

Page 21 Happy Bird-day
MATERIALS
Stamps: Memory Box—B291 Big Chick, B282 Sparkler, AA287 Hat, and C212 Happy Birthday

Cardstock: White; Rubber Soul—Aqua

Note card: Rubber Soul—Wave

Colored pencils: Prismacolor—918 Orange, 916 Canary Yellow, and 1002 Yellowed Orange

Ink: Tsukineko—VersaFine Onyx Black and VersaMagic Sea Breeze

Sponge dauber

Sewing machine and white thread

Glitter glue

HOW TO:

Stamp the bird, hat, and sparkler with black ink onto white cardstock. Add a layer of Orange at the bottom edge of the bird, fading upward ¼". Blend over the Orange and the rest of the bird with Canary Yellow. For the hat, begin with a layer of Orange at the bottom of the hat and fade upward. Add a layer of Yellowed Orange over the hat to blend, pressing hard. Color the center of the sparkler Canary Yellow and add glitter glue. Cut the image to size and sponge the edges with Sea Breeze. Mount the image onto the Aqua cardstock and stitch a border around the edges. Mount the piece onto the Wave note card and stamp "happy birthday" in black.

Page 22
Filigree Bouquet
MATERIALS

Stamp: Memory Box—E190 Mixed Bouquet

White cardstock

Note card: Rubber Soul—Aqua

Colored pencils: Prismacolor—916 Canary Yellow, 918 Orange, 1002 Yellowed Orange, and 926 Carmine Red

Ink: Tsukineko—VersaFine Onyx Black and VersaMagic Sea Breeze

Decorative paper clip

Sponge or sponge dauber

HOW TO:

Stamp the mixed bouquet onto white cardstock with black ink. For the smaller flowers, color the petals solid with yellows or oranges. For the larger flowers, add a soft layer of Orange around the centers, leaving uncolored areas around the edges of the petals. Add a layer of Yellowed Orange over the Orange and the rest of each flower. Using a sharp pencil, add Carmine Red to the centers of the larger flowers. Trim the image to size and cut a second piece of white cardstock to match. Sponge Sea Breeze ink around the edge of the image. Layer and adhere the image to the second piece of white cardstock. Then mount the layered piece onto the note card. Glue the paper clip in place.

Page 22 Floating Petals
MATERIALS
Stamp: Memory Box—B692 Violet

Cardstock: White; Rubber Soul—Wave

Note card: Rubber Soul—Aqua

Colored pencils: Prismacolor—1100 China

Blue, 1103 Caribbean Sea, 904 Cerulean Blue, 1087 Powder Blue, 918 Orange, 1002 Yellowed Orange, 917 Sunburst Yellow, 989 Chartreuse, and 916 Canary Yellow

Ink: Tsukineko—VersaFine Onyx Black

HOW TO:

Stamp the flower onto white cardstock with black ink as shown. For a blue color scheme, begin with a layer of China Blue at the outer tip of each petal, fading toward the center. Next add a layer of Caribbean Sea, overlapping the China Blue and extending along the sides of each petal, fading toward the center. Add a layer of Cerulean Blue on top of that, and then Powder Blue, with each color fading a little more toward the center but still leaving some white space near the center. Finally blend over the entire petal with Powder Blue, pressing hard, but avoiding the darkest areas at the tip of each petal. For an orange color scheme, begin with Orange near the center on each petal, fading outward. Add a layer of Yellowed Orange and fade it a little further toward the outer edges of the petals. Blend over each petal with Sunburst Yellow, pressing hard. For the centers, use the Chartreuse pencil to draw a small crescent line of green along one edge of each circular center. Fill in the rest of the center with Canary Yellow, overlapping the green.

Page 23 Bon Voyage
MATERIALS
Stamp: Memory Box—B635 Suitcase

Cardstock: Memory Box—Peapod

White note card

Colored pencils: Prismacolor—956 Lilac, 934 Lavender, 993 Hot Pink, 911 Olive Green, 1005 Limepeel, 926 Carmine Red, 1103 Caribbean Sea, 1087 Powder Blue, 989 Chartreuse, 906 Copenhagen Blue, 918 Orange, 916 Canary Yellow, 993 Hot Pink, 1018 Pink Rose, 1002 Yellowed Orange, 917 Sunburst Yellow, 994 Process Red, 923 Scarlet Lake, and 913 Spring Green

Ink: Tsukineko—VersaFine Onyx Black

Ruler

One 7" length each of ⅜"-wide olive and brown ribbons

Small buckle: Li'l Davis Designs

HOW TO:

Stamp the suitcase vertically along the note card as shown, masking one of the suitcases. For the top suitcase, begin with a soft line of

Lilac around the inside edges of the image and along the middle straps. Add a layer of Lavender over the Lilac, coloring softly so that the paper shows though the color slightly. Color the straps of the case Hot Pink. For the second suitcase, begin with a soft line of Olive Green around the inside edges of the shape and around the straps. Add a soft layer of Limepeel over the Olive Green. Color the straps with Carmine Red, pressing hard. Use a ruler and sharpened Scarlet Lake, Spring Green, and Limepeel pencils to create cross-hatched lines. For the third suitcase, begin with a soft line of Caribbean Sea around the inside edges and straps of the suitcase. Add a layer of Powder Blue over the first layer, coloring softly. Color the straps Chartreuse. Using a ruler and a sharpened Copenhagen Blue pencil, add broken lines across the width of the suitcase. For the fourth suitcase, begin with a soft line of Orange around the inside edges and straps of the image. Add a layer of Canary Yellow on top of the Orange, coloring softly. Color the straps Orange, pressing firmly. For the last suitcase, begin with a soft line of Hot Pink around the inside edges and straps. Add a layer of Pink Rose over the Hot Pink, coloring softly. Color in the straps with a blend of Yellowed Orange (first layer) and Sunburst Yellow (blending layer). With a sharpened Process Red pencil and a ruler, add lines to create a mesh pattern. Adhere a border of Peapod cardstock to the left side of the note card and secure the two ribbons over the right edge of the cardstock, installing the buckle on the brown ribbon.

Page 23 Girls' Night Out
MATERIALS
Stamps: Memory Box—B668 Prom Dress, B670 Slip Dress, and B672 Evening Dress

Cardstock: White; Memory Box—Currant

Patterned paper: Memory Box—Sugar Collection

Note card: Memory Box—Gourd

Colored pencils: Prismacolor—926 Carmine Red, 994 Process Red, 993 Hot Pink, 918 Orange, 1002 Yellowed Orange, and 917 Sunburst Yellow

Ink: Tsukineko—VersaFine Onyx Black

Ruler

HOW TO:

Stamp the three dresses onto white cardstock with black ink. Shade the sides of the left and center dresses with Carmine Red, fading toward the centers. For the dress on the left, add a layer of Process Red over the Carmine Red and fade further toward the center. Add a final layer of Hot Pink, coloring heavily at the sides and fading to a soft layer in the center. With a sharpened Process Red pencil, draw lines across the dress. For the dress in the middle, add a layer of Orange over the Carmine Red layer, fading toward the center of the image. Next add a layer of Yellowed Orange, fading toward the center. Add a final layer of Sunburst Yellow, pressing hard over the entire dress. With a sharpened Orange pencil and a ruler, draw diagonal lines across the dress. For the dress on the right, lightly draw tiny circles with Carmine Red. Avoid coloring inside the circles. Begin on the left and right sides of the dress with a layer of Process Red, avoiding the circles and fading toward the center. Add a final blending layer of Carmine Red over the Process Red, coloring in the dress while still avoiding the circles. Trim, layer, and mount the papers to the card.

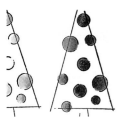

Page 24 Prismatic Christmas Trees

MATERIALS

Stamp: Memory Box—CS-106 Oh Christmas Tree Set

White note card

Colored pencils: Prismacolor—989 Chartreuse, 916 Canary Yellow, 917 Sunburst Yellow, 1002 Yellowed Orange, 926 Carmine Red, 994 Process Red, 934 Lavender, 903 True Blue, 1024 Blue Slate, and 1087 Powder Blue

Ink: Tsukineko—VersaFine Onyx Black

HOW TO:

Stamp the Christmas tree three times onto the white note card with black ink. Begin on the left side with Chartreuse, coloring hard at first and fading halfway across three or four of the bubbles. Add a layer of Canary Yellow over the Chartreuse and press hard to blend. Moving right, add a layer of Sunburst Yellow on the right side of two or three bubbles and then add a layer of Canary Yellow on top of the Sunburst Yellow. Continue moving across the card, adding blends of color in the order specified in the materials list, ending with a blend of Blue Slate and Powder Blue.

Page 24 Heartfelt Greetings

MATERIALS

Stamps: Memory Box—D719 Loving Snowman and B726 Heartfelt Greetings

White cardstock

Note card: Memory Box—Cranberry

Colored pencils: Prismacolor—1024 Blue Slate, 1087 Powder Blue, 923 Scarlet Lake, 918 Orange, 1018 Pink Rose, 911 Olive Green, 1005 Limepeel, and 1002 Sunburst Yellow

Ink: Tsukineko—VersaFine Onyx Black

HOW TO:

Stamp the snowman and "heartfelt greetings" onto white cardstock with black ink. Shade the left side of the snowman with Blue Slate, working softly in a crescent shape along the curves. Overlap the Blue Slate with a soft layer of Powder Blue, adding just a little more pressure near the edges of the curves. Color the hearts with Scarlet Lake, pressing firmly. Color the nose Orange and add a soft circle of Pink Rose on the cheeks of the snowman. For the scarf, begin with a soft line of Olive Green along the edges. Color over the Olive Green with a soft layer of Limepeel, and then Sunburst Yellow. With a sharpened Scarlet Lake pencil, add plaid lines for pattern over the green layers. Cut the cardstock to size and mount to the note card.

Page 24 Snowman at Sunset

MATERIALS

Stamp: Memory Box—D321 Snowman Scene

Cardstock: Memory Box—Water

Note card: Rubber Soul—Hydrangea

Colored pencils: Prismacolor—1005 Limepeel, 989 Chartreuse, 1102 Blue Lake, 903 True Blue, 1087 Powder Blue, 993 Hot Pink, 995 Mulberry, and 956 Lilac

Ink: Tsukineko—Brilliance Graphite Black

White shrink plastic

Diamond glaze: JudiKins

Fine-grit sandpaper

HOW TO:

Sand the white shrink plastic to create some "tooth" for the colored pencil to grab onto. Stamp the snowman scene with black ink and let dry overnight. Color the trees on one side with Limepeel, fading toward the center. Color over the Limepeel and across the remaining area with Chartreuse to blend. Color in the hat with Blue Lake. Blend across the sky, beginning on the left with True Blue, followed by Blue Lake, Powder Blue, Hot Pink, Mulberry, and Lilac last. Overlap the colors as you move across the sky, using light colors for blending the transitional areas. Add stripes on the scarf with Chartreuse and Hot Pink. Cut the image out of the sheet of shrink plastic. Heat the image following the manufacturer's instructions. Add a layer of diamond glaze over the shrunken piece and let dry overnight. Cut the

Water cardstock slightly smaller than the note card and mount to the card front. Mount the shrink-plastic image to the card.

Page 24 Miniature Peony Tile

MATERIALS

Stamp: Memory Box—D298 Flower Portrait

Patterned paper: Memory Box—Homespun Collection

Note card: Rubber Soul—Periwinkle

Colored pencils: Prismacolor—994 Process Red, 993 Hot Pink, 1005 Limepeel, 911 Olive Green, 989 Chartreuse, 1102 Blue Lake, and 1087 Powder Blue

Ink: Tsukineko—Brilliance Graphite Black

White shrink plastic

Fine-grit sandpaper

HOW TO:

Sand the white shrink plastic, stamp the flower image with black ink, and let dry overnight. Shade each petal of the flower, beginning with Process Red near the center and fading away from the center. Blend over each petal with Hot Pink. Color the stem with Limepeel. Add a layer of Olive Green near the base of each leaf and fade toward the top of the leaf. Add a layer of Limepeel beginning at the bottom of the leaves and fading a little further up. Add a final blending layer, coloring hard over the entire leaf with Chartreuse. Color in the background with Blue Lake, leaving a small amount of uncolored area around the stem, leaves, and petals. Add Powder Blue in the uncolored area and blend it with firm pressure into the Blue Lake. Cut out the image and shrink according to the manufacturer's instructions. Cut the patterned paper slightly smaller than the note card and mount to the card front. Mount the shrink-plastic image to the card.

Page 25 A Simple Bouquet blue-on-blue scheme

MATERIALS

Stamp: Memory Box—E269 Scribble Bouquet

Cold press watercolor paper

Note card: Memory Box—Blue Poppy

Colored pencils: Prismacolor—989 Chartreuse, 918 Orange, and 916 Canary Yellow

Ink: Tsukineko—VersaFine Onyx Black

Watercolor paint

HOW TO:

Create a wash of blue and green watercolor paint on the watercolor paper (see "Watercolor Basics" on page 26) and let dry completely. Stamp the bouquet onto watercolor paper with black ink. Color the stems and leaves with Chartreuse. Shade the flowers with Orange, beginning on any side and fading quickly toward the center, allowing the texture to show. Blend over the Orange and the rest of the flower with Canary Yellow. Tear the edges of the watercolor paper and mount it to the card.

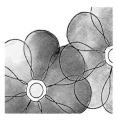

Page 28
Pinwheel Posy
MATERIALS

Stamp: Impress—2092D Outline Posey

Cold press watercolor paper

Cardstock: Memory Box—Peony

Note card: Memory Box—Mango

Watercolor pencils: Faber-Castell Albrecht Durer—142 Madder, 121 Pale Geranium Lake, 133 Magenta, 124 Rose Carmine, 109 Dark Chrome Yellow, 107 Cadmium Yellow, and 171 Light Green

Ink: Tsukineko—VersaFine Onyx Black

Watercolor brush

HOW TO:

Refer to the photo on page 28 for color application before blending.

Stamp the flower image onto watercolor paper three times with black ink, overlapping as shown on page 28. Let dry completely. Shade the petals with the red, orange, and yellow pencils, leaving spaces between the areas of color for paler areas. To set up a blend, overlap areas of color slightly. With a wet paint brush, begin painting the lighter colors until they dissolve and gradually move around the images, keeping the brush on the surface as much as possible. Add more water as necessary. Allow the petals to dry before painting the center with the Light Green pencil. Trim, layer, and mount the papers to the card.

Page 29   Three Trees in a Row
MATERIALS

Stamp: Rubbermoon—GE2662H Tree

Cold press watercolor paper

Cardstock: Memory Box—Key Lime and Mango

Watercolor paints: Winsor & Newton Cotman—Sap Green, Lemon Yellow Hue, and Cadmium Orange

Ink: Tsukineko—VersaMagic Jumbo Java

Watercolor brush

HOW TO:

Refer to the photo on page 29 for color application before blending.

Stamp the tree three times with Jumbo Java ink onto watercolor paper as shown on page 29. Let dry completely. Paint a circle over the tree branches with plain water, wait for a minute, and repeat. Load the brush with Sap Green paint and add to one side of the wet circle. Rinse and load the brush with Lemon Yellow Hue, and then paint the opposite side of the circle. Drag the yellow into the green and then back to the center. Repeat a few times until color is mixed in the center. If the color is not blended enough, rinse and dry the brush, and then rub the slightly damp brush over the areas of mixed color to even out any hard lines. Use the brush to add a small amount of Orange paint to the edge of the circle. Let dry. Trim the tree images to size and mount onto Mango cardstock. Trim a scant ⅛" from the edge of the watercolor paper. Mount onto Key Lime cardstock and trim 1⁄16" from the edge of the Mango cardstock. Mount onto another piece of Mango cardstock and trim a scant ⅛" from the Key Lime cardstock. Mount the bordered design to the card.

Page 30   Vivid Vases
MATERIALS

Stamp: Rubbermoon—GE2573E Vase

Cold press watercolor paper

Cardstock: Memory Box—Sugar Plum

Note card: Memory Box—Peony

Watercolor markers: Marvy Le Plume II—43 Brilliant Yellow, 94 Scarlet, 52 Yellow Green, 9 Pink, 100 Sapphire, and 96 Jungle Green

Ink: Tsukineko—Brilliance Graphite Black

Foam mounting squares

Watercolor brush

HOW TO:

Refer to the photo on page 30 for color application before blending.

Stamp the vase three times with black ink onto watercolor paper as shown on page 30. Let dry. Color the vase and the berries on the branches with Brilliant Yellow. Color the center of the roses with Scarlet and color the leaves with Yellow Green. Add Pink to the top of the vases, on top of the Brilliant Yellow. Add a spot of Sapphire beneath the vases. With a wet paintbrush, rub over the vases until the pink and yellow areas are blended—about three or four strokes. Rinse the brush and pull the Scarlet color over the rose blooms. Rinse and fill the leaves and berries in by pulling the color around the images. While the paper is still wet, add Jungle Green to the top of each leaf and blend into the lighter green color. Rinse the brush and dissolve the Sapphire under the vases by rubbing over the blue areas until the color spreads. Trim the painted images to size and mount onto Sugar Plum cardstock with foam squares. Trim a scant ⅛" from the edges of the watercolor paper. Mount the image to the card.

Page 31   Harvest Wreath
MATERIALS

Stamp: Memory Box—C140 Oak Wreath

Cold press watercolor paper

Cardstock: Memory Box—Mango

Note card: Memory Box—Jack O Lantern

Watercolor pencils: Faber-Castell Albrecht Durer—168 Earth Green Yellowish, 171 Light Green, 107 Cadmium Yellow, 115 Dark Cadmium Orange, and 121 Pale Geranium Lake

Ink: Tsukineko—VersaFine Vintage Sepia

6" length of ⅛"-wide black-and-copper metallic ribbon

Watercolor brush

HOW TO:

Refer to the photo on page 31 for color application before blending.

Stamp the wreath onto watercolor paper with Vintage Sepia and let dry. Softly color with Earth Green Yellowish and Light Green in patches around the outside of the leaves, overlapping the two greens randomly. Load a brush with water and wet the area inside the wreath and near the outside of the green areas around the wreath. Add water until the paper appears evenly wet. Pull water from the wet areas into the green pigment and then back out, using a swirling motion and keeping the brush on the paper at all times. Move around the wreath, dissolving all the green areas and adding more water as necessary. Let dry completely. Color half of each leaf Cadmium Yellow and the other half Dark Cadmium Orange. Add a small amount of Pale Geranium Lake to the bottom of each leaf over the orange area. Load a brush (No. 2 or No. 4 round) with water and wet each leaf, beginning in the light area and swirling toward the dark areas. Let dry completely. Trim the image to size and mount onto Mango cardstock. Trim the layered image to size and wrap a length of ribbon around each corner, taping the ribbon to the back. Mount the image to the card.

Page 31   Oriental Poppy
MATERIALS

Stamp: Memory Box—F703 Open Poppy

Cold press watercolor paper

Cardstock: Memory Box—Mango

Note card: Memory Box—Holly Berry

Watercolor pencils: Faber-Castell Albrecht Durer—107 Cadmium Yellow, 111 Cadmium Orange, and 142 Madder

Ink: Tsukineko—VersaFine Onyx Black

Watercolor brush

HOW TO:

Refer to the photo on page 31 for color application before blending.

Stamp the poppy onto watercolor paper with black ink and let dry. Apply Cadmium Yellow inside each petal near the center, leaving approximately ½" from the tip of each petal white. Shade half of the remaining white space with Cadmium Orange, slightly overlapping into the yellow area. Finish coloring in the empty space with Madder. Repeat this process for each petal, changing the size for each colored area slightly so that each petal has a distinct look. Load a brush with plain water and begin painting in the center, moving toward the outer edge of the petals, but keeping the brush on the surface of the paper the whole time. If the brush begins to dry (meaning the pencil will not dissolve), move the brush to the side of the petal and lift it off the paper. Load the brush with water again and resume where you lifted the brush from the paper, continuing toward the outer edge of the petals. Once the outer edge is reached, lift the brush from the paper. If desired, pull a bit of the darker colors toward the center of the flower. To pull color while the paint is still wet, rinse the brush in clear water and dry it on a paper towel so that the brush hairs are only slightly damp. Press the brush into the darker area, move down into the lighter area, and then move back into the darker area in a circular motion. Repeat a few times and then lift off the paper when back in the darker area. Trim, layer, and mount the papers to the card.

Page 32   Tea Time
MATERIALS

Stamp: Lockhart Stamp Company—2020 Teapot

Cold press watercolor paper

Patterned paper: Memory Box—Homespun Collection

Note card: Memory Box—Paprika

Watercolor pencils: Faber-Castell Albrecht Durer—190 Venetian Red, 185 Light Ochre, 115 Dark Cadmium Orange, 217 Middle Cadmium Red, 129 Pink Madder Lake, 107 Cadmium Yellow, and 126 Permanent Carmine

Ink: Tsukineko—Brilliance Graphite Black

Watercolor brush

HOW TO:

Stamp the image with black ink onto watercolor paper and let dry. Color in the border with patches of Venetian Red, Light Ochre, and Dark Cadmium Orange, and then wet with a brush, swirling the brush along the border. Color the entire teapot in Light Ochre, then shade the bottom of the teapot lightly with Middle Cadmium Red. Blend with a wet brush. Add a small amount of Pink Madder Lake at the bottom of the napkin, and then use a wet brush to pull color across the rest of the napkin. Color in the saucer, lemon wedges, and plate with Cadmium Yellow. Wet these areas to dissolve the color. For the background behind the teapot, color the corners heavily with Permanent Carmine and then fill in the rest of the background very lightly. Apply a wet brush to the background, swirling just long enough to dissolve the pencil pigment. Then move on so that the pigment stays strong in the corners without getting too diluted. Do the same with the tablecloth, applying Dark Cadmium Orange heavily at the bottom. Wet the orange areas with a brush briefly, just enough to dissolve them, and then stop. Apply color to the remaining portions of the image in the same manner. Trim the image to size and cut slightly larger squares from the patterned papers. Mount the layers of patterned paper and the painted image to the note card at angles.

Page 33   A Gift for You
MATERIALS

Stamp: Hero Arts—E3773 Polka Dot Present

Hot press watercolor paper

Note card: Memory Box—Key Lime

Watercolor pencils: Faber-Castell Albrecht Durer—104 Light Yellow Glaze, 171 Light Green, 156 Cobalt Green, and 111 Cadmium Orange

Ink: Tsukineko—VersaFine Onyx Black and VersaColor Lime; Impress—Fresh Ink Island

Watercolor brush

HOW TO:

Stamp the image with black ink onto watercolor paper and let dry. Lightly shade in the entire present with Light Yellow Glaze. Shade the left side of the present with a layer of Light Green directly on top of the yellow. Add a small amount of Light Green to the right edge of the present. Load a brush with water and use a gentle swirling motion to work along the front of the present, from left to right. Lift the brush only when the front is completely filled in. Rinse the brush to eliminate any green paint left in the brush hairs and then paint the top of the present, dissolving all the yellow pigment. Let dry. Load the brush with water and wet the left side of the present, beginning at the top and working the brush downward in a back-and-forth motion, filling the area with a yellowish green mixture. Let dry completely. Once the image is dry, trace over the ribbon strings with Cobalt Green and fill in all the dots with Cadmium Orange. Leave the Cobalt Green and Cadmium Orange dry, because adding water may cause them to spread too much. Trim the image to size. Place the image on a sheet of scrap paper and load a dauber with Island ink and a second dauber with Lime ink. Using a circular motion and beginning on the scrap paper, swirl the Island dauber onto the edges of the watercolor paper. Switch to the Lime dauber and swirl along the edge on top of the Island areas. Mount the watercolor piece to the card. Glue ⅛"-wide strips of patterned paper over the corners of the watercolor piece.

Page 33   Fruits of Labor
MATERIALS

Stamp: Lockhart Stamp Company—2029 Fruitbowl

Cold press watercolor paper

Note card: Rubber Soul—Periwinkle

Colored pencils: Faber-Castell Albrecht Durer—107 Cadmium Yellow, 171 Light Green, 156 Cobalt Green, 120 Ultramarine, 140 Light Ultramarine, 136 Purple Violet, 142 Madder, 115 Dark Cadmium Orange, and 185 Light Ochre

Ink: Tsukineko—Brilliance Graphite Black

Watercolor brush

HOW TO:

Stamp the image with black ink onto water-color paper and let dry completely. Color the outermost border Cobalt Green, leaving open spaces every ¼" or so. Wet the area with a brush, allowing strong areas and weak areas to develop without brushing the color too much. Color the inner border with a soft layer of Cadmium Yellow and add a couple patches of Light Green randomly on the yellow layer. Wet with a brush and dissolve the green and yellow areas together. Color in the background around the fruit bowl with over-lapping areas of Cobalt Green, Ultramarine, and Light Ultramarine, concentrating most of the pressure along the edges and corners of the background. Wet the colored areas with a brush, working in the edges and corners and pulling the color toward the center. Draw small circles on the bowl with Cobalt Green and fill in the rest of the bowl around the Cobalt Green. Wet the green areas of the bowl, avoiding the uncolored white circles. Let dry completely. Color the stripe on the bowl with Cadmium Yellow and let dry. Color five or six grapes with Purple Violet, and then wet to dissolve. Use the purple pigment remaining on the brush to color in the rest of the grapes. Color the apples with Madder, pressing heavily so that no white watercolor paper shows through. With a slightly damp brush, dissolve the Madder color to give the apple shapes a thick, rich look. Repeat with Cadmium Yellow for the lemon and Dark Cadmium Orange for the oranges. Color the pear a solid layer of light Ochre and add a light shading of Dark Cadmium Orange at the bottom of the shape. Dissolve the color on the pear with a damp brush. Fill in the leaves with Light Green and wet each leaf with a damp paintbrush. Allow the watercolor piece to dry, and then cut it out and mount it onto a couple layers of scrap cardstock cut slightly smaller. This will give the image some depth. Mount the image to the card.

Page 33 All Bundled Up

MATERIALS

Stamp: Lockhart Stamp Company—6003 Snowman with Bird

Cold press watercolor paper

Cardstock: Rubber Soul—Hydrangea and Marina

Note card: Rubber Soul—Wave

Watercolor pencils: Faber-Castell Albrecht Durer—120 Ultramarine, 105 Light Cadmium Yellow, 171 Light Green, 156 Cobalt Green, 107 Phthalo Blue, and 115 Dark Cadmium Orange, and 129 Pink Madder Lake

Ink: Tsukineko—Brilliance Graphite Black

Watercolor brush

HOW TO:

Stamp the image with black ink onto water-color paper and let dry. Color in the border with Ultramarine, leaving open spaces every ½" or so. Wet the Ultramarine with a paint-brush, dissolving the color all around the border and allowing strong and weak areas of color to develop without smoothing over them too much. With Ultramarine still left on the brush, paint around the snowflakes in the back-ground around the snowman. If the brush runs out of paint, rewet it, paint over the border a little bit to pick up some more paint, and continue filling in the background. If the back-ground appears uneven, rinse the brush and paint over the background, avoiding the areas around the snowflakes but keeping the brush on the paper to smooth out hard lines of color. The background should appear very pale. Color the left and right sides of the snowman hat with Ultramarine. Wet the brush and pull color toward the center of the hat. With the paint remaining on the brush, paint the sides of the snowman's face and outline his earmuffs so that a soft blue shadow develops. Color the scarf with Light Cadmium Yellow and shade around the knot of the scarf with Cobalt Green and Light Green. Wet the brush and dissolve the color on the scarf, beginning at the yellow areas and ending at the green, working until the color has dissolved smoothly. Color in the coat stripes with Phthalo Blue and wet them with the brush. With leftover Phthalo Blue, paint in the polka-dot area of the hat, avoid-ing the circles. Add Light Cadmium Yellow to the birdie on the hat and to the area around the buttons on his coat. Add Dark Cadmium Orange to the carrot nose and wet with the brush. Touch the tip of the Pink Madder Lake pencil with a clean, wet brush and rub a little pink onto the cheek areas of the face. Let dry. Cut rectangles from Marina and Hydrangea cardstock and mount to the front of the note card as shown. Cut the image out of water-color paper and mount to the card.

Page 34 Dancing Butterflies

MATERIALS

Stamp: Savvy Stamps—608C Stripe Sketch Butterfly

Cardstock: White; Memory Box—Eggshell, Flax, Cantaloupe, Peony, and Sherbet

Note card: Memory Box—Sweet Corn

Watercolor pencils: Faber-Castell Albrecht Durer—108 Dark Cadmium Yellow, 111 Cadmium Orange, 115 Dark Cadmium Orange, and 126 Permanent Carmine

Ink: Tsukineko—Brilliance Graphite Black and VersaMagic Gingerbread

Watercolor brush

HOW TO:

Stamp two butterfly images onto Eggshell card-stock with black ink. Stamp two more images onto white cardstock with Gingerbread and let dry completely. With a wet paintbrush, rub the tip of the Dark Cadmium Yellow pencil until the brush is loaded with paint. Paint a solid layer of yellow over the wings of one butter-fly. Repeat, applying a second thick layer of yellow paint. Load a brush with Cadmium Orange and apply to the tips of the butterfly wings over the yellow layers. Rinse the brush and dry it slightly so that it is still damp. Rub the orange into the yellow area in a gentle swirling or back-and-forth motion until the color is smooth. Rinse the brush and rub the tip of the Dark Cadmium Orange pencil until the brush is loaded with paint. Apply to the wings of the second butterfly. Repeat, adding a second layer of Dark Cadmium Orange to the wings. Switch to the Permanent Carmine pencil, rubbing the tip of the pencil until the brush is loaded with paint. Apply Permanent Carmine over the orange at the tips of the wings. Rinse the brush and dry until slightly damp. Rub the Permanent Carmine into the orange area gently until smooth.

Cut out the painted butterflies and bend the wings slightly. Mount the butterflies onto the Eggshell cardstock, lining up the images and allowing the wings to lift off the surface. Trim, layer, and mount the Eggshell and Flax papers to the card. Cut a total of 20 freehand squares from the Cantaloupe, Peony, and Sherbet papers and glue them around the border of the card.

Page 34 Wedding Congratulations

MATERIALS

Stamp: Savvy Stamps—473C Scalloped Wedding Cake

Cardstock: Memory Box—Eggshell, Sweet Corn, Key Lime, Cantaloupe, Sherbet, and Peony

White note card

Watercolor pencils: Faber-Castell Albrecht Durer—124 Rose Carmine and 109 Dark Chrome Yellow

Watercolor marker: Marvy Le Plume II—94 Scarlet

Ink: Tsukineko—Brilliance Graphite Black

¼" circle punch

Watercolor brush

HOW TO:

Apply black ink to the stamp image. With a wet paper towel, remove the ink from the rubber that defines the heart on top of the cake. Color the heart with Scarlet and stamp the image onto Eggshell cardstock. Let dry completely. With a wet paint brush, rub the tip of the Rose Carmine pencil until the brush is loaded with pink paint. Apply the brush to the left side of the scalloped area, keeping the brush on the paper and working toward the right in a gentle swirling motion. The color will fade out as you approach the right side. Reapply pink paint to the brush from the tip of the pencil and apply to the left side of the cake, working the brush toward the right. Lift the brush off the paper once the cake is filled in. Rinse and rub the tip of the brush on the Dark Chrome Yellow pencil, loading the brush with paint. Apply the yellow over the pink, beginning at the left side of the cake and ending on the right. Let dry. Trim, layer, and mount the Eggshell and Sweet Corn papers to the card. Punch four ¼" circles each from Key Lime, Cantaloupe, Sherbet, and Peony and glue the circles around the mounted layers.

Page 35 Berry Branches
MATERIALS

Stamp: Impress—2089C Dotted Branch

Hot press watercolor paper

Cardstock: Memory Box—Moss

Note card: Memory Box—Eggshell

Watercolor pencils: Faber-Castell Albrecht Durer—107 Cadmium Yellow, 219 Deep Scarlet Red, 125 Middle Purple Pink, 115 Dark Cadmium Orange, 109 Dark Chrome Yellow, and 168 Earth Green Yellowish

Ink: Tsukineko—Brilliance Graphite Black

Watercolor brush

HOW TO:

To make a wash of color for the background, wet a rectangular area of the watercolor paper (approximately 3" by 4") by brushing plain water onto the surface until saturated. Allow to rest for a minute, and then reapply water. Draw a thick line of Cadmium Yellow on the paper around the wet area. With a wet brush, pull the yellow into the wet area, working in a back-and-forth swirling motion from the top to the bottom and keeping the brush on the paper constantly. If the brush runs out

of liquid, pull the brush to the side of the wet area and lift off the paper. Rewet the brush and begin again at the area you lifted from. Allow the background to dry completely. Cut the paper down so that any remaining yellow line surrounding the rectangle is no longer visible.

Stamp the dotted branch onto the painted watercolor paper with black ink and let dry. Working from the tip of the pencil, load the brush with Deep Scarlet Red and paint over the tips of some of the berry images, distributing the color evenly among the branches. Repeat with the remaining pencil colors (except green), until all the berries are colored. Let dry. With a clean, wet brush, pick up color from the tip of the Earth Green Yellowish pencil and paint along all the stem lines. Let dry, and then trim, layer, and mount the papers to the card.

Page 35 A New Nest
MATERIALS

Stamps: Savvy Stamps—793E Two Birds in Nest and 794B A New Nest

Cardstock: Memory Box—Eggshell and Peapod

Patterned paper: Memory Box—12" x 12" Sugar (Beads)

Watercolor pencils: Faber-Castell Albrecht Durer—107 Cadmium Yellow, 283 Burnt Sienna, and 171 Light Green

Ink: Tsukineko—VersaFine Onyx Black and VersaMagic Jumbo Java and Gingerbread

7" length of ⅛"-wide brown grosgrain ribbon

½", ¼", and ⅛" circle punches

Sewing machine and ecru thread

Sponge or sponge dauber

Watercolor brush

HOW TO:

Cut the Eggshell cardstock into a tag shape. Punch out a ½" Peapod circle and a ¼" Eggshell circle, then layer them over the top of the tag, securing in place. Punch a ⅛" hole in the center of the layered circles to create a hole reinforcement. Stamp the nest image with black ink onto the top of the tag. Working with a wet brush, rub the tip of the Cadmium Yellow pencil until the brush is loaded with paint. Fill in the birds in one pass, taking care not to oversaturate the cardstock with liquid (which may cause warping). Rinse the brush and rub the tip of the Burnt Sienna pencil, filling the brush with paint. Brush over the nest

and branch area. Rinse the brush and rub the tip of the Light Green pencil until the brush is loaded with paint. Paint green over the leaf shapes, allowing the brush to go outside the lines if desired. Stamp the phrase "a new nest" in Jumbo Java ink underneath nest image. Let dry completely. Holding the tag shape in one hand, use the other hand to brush the sides of the tag with the Gingerbread inkpad and set aside to dry.

To make a pocket, cut the patterned paper to size to make a back piece and a front piece (pieces should be slightly larger than the tag). Trim the front piece to expose the stamped image on the tag. Apply Gingerbread ink to the edges of the pieces with a dauber or sponge. Create a layered front band by cutting a strip of Eggshell paper slightly narrower than a strip of Peapod paper. Apply Gingerbread ink to the edges of the Eggshell strip and mount onto the Peapod strip. Mount the layered strip to the pocket front piece. Layer the front over the back, right sides facing up, and use a zigzag stitch along the edges to secure. Tie the ribbon through the hole in the tag and insert the tag into the pocket.

Page 36 Spring Tree
MATERIALS

Stamp: Impress—3004D Bare Tree

Hot press watercolor paper

Cardstock: White

Note card: Memory Box—Endive

Watercolor paints: Winsor & Newton Cotman—Sap Green, Cobalt Blue, and Lemon Yellow Hue

Ink: Tsukineko—Brilliance Graphite Black

Watercolor brush

HOW TO:

Stamp the tree with black ink onto watercolor paper and let dry. Load a brush with Sap Green paint and create a hill shape under the tree. Areas of light and dark color will naturally develop; allow these to remain without over-working them. Let the hill area dry completely before proceeding. Load a brush with Cobalt Blue paint and paint the outer edges of the sky, working quickly with the brush constantly on the paper and slowly moving toward the center around the tree (don't paint inside the branches). Crackly or patchy areas will develop with this dry technique, which adds visual interest. Once the sky is dry, load the brush with Lemon Yellow Hue and paint a circle of color over the tree branches. While still wet, add Sap Green to the yellow area. Rinse and dry the brush, and then mix the green and yellow areas together with a gentle swirling figure-eight motion. Trim, layer, and mount the papers to the card.

Page 36   Winter Tree at Sunset
MATERIALS
Stamp: Impress—3004D Bare Tree

Hot press watercolor paper

Cardstock: Memory Box—Crimson

Note card: Memory Box—Mango

Watercolor paints: Winsor & Newton Cotman—Cadmium Yellow Pale, Cadmium Orange, Alizarin Crimson, and Cadmium Red

Ink: Tsukineko—Brilliance Graphite Black

Watercolor brush

HOW TO:
Brush plain water over a 3" x 3" area of watercolor paper and allow to set for a minute. Reapply water over the same area so that paper is saturated. Load a brush with Cadmium Yellow Pale paint. Touch the brush to the upper-left corner of the wet paper to test whether the paint will run. If it doesn't spread, the paper is too dry and you'll need to apply more water. If paint fills the whole wet area quickly and becomes very pale, there is too much water on the surface, and it should dry a little. If the paint begins to fill in a little, the paper is sufficiently wet. Keeping the brush on the paper, gently massage the color across the wet area in a back-and-forth figure-eight motion, working from the top to the bottom. The yellow will become fainter as the pigment runs out. Rinse the brush and load it with Cadmium Orange.

For the sky, apply the brush to the upper-left corner and move across the top, keeping the brush constantly on the paper. Paint only about 1/2" down from the top, and then move the brush to the side and lift it off the paper. If the orange seems to dissolve well into the yellow area, leave it to dry. If the orange doesn't seem to be doing anything, rinse the brush and dry the bristles on a paper towel until they are just slightly damp. Use the brush to rub in a circular motion over the line between the orange and yellow areas until smooth. Rinse and dry the brush and repeat as needed. Let dry completely.

For the hill, load the brush with Alizarin Crimson paint and create an arched area across the sky near the bottom of the wet area. While the hill is still wet, load the brush with Cadmium Red and trace along the top of the arch with this darker color. If needed, fade the darker red into the lighter red with a clean, slightly damp brush. Let dry completely.

Stamp the tree onto the watercolor paper with black ink so that the bottom of the tree rests on the hill. Trim, layer, and mount the papers to the card.

**Page 37
Embossed Resist
Daisies**
MATERIALS
Stamps: Memory Box—CS-103 Scribble Flower Set

Cold press watercolor paper

Cardstock: Memory Box—Blueberry

Note card: Memory Box—Meadow

Watercolor paints: Winsor & Newton Cotman—Cobalt Blue, Intense (Phthalo) Blue, and Lemon Yellow Hue

Ink: Tsukineko—VersaMark

Clear embossing powder

Watercolor brush

HOW TO:
Stamp the flower several times onto watercolor paper with VersaMark ink and emboss with clear powder. Wet the watercolor paper with plain water and allow it to set for a minute. Reapply water to ensure the surface is saturated. Load a brush with Cobalt Blue paint and apply to half of the wet area, avoiding the centers of the flowers. Rinse and load the brush with Intense (Phthalo) Blue and apply to the other half of the wet area, avoiding the centers of the flowers and slightly overlapping the Cobalt Blue areas. Rinse and load the brush with Lemon Yellow Hue and apply to the centers of the flowers. Let dry completely, and then trim, layer, and mount the papers to the card.

**Page 37
Modern Trees**
MATERIALS
Stamps: Memory Box—B229 3/4" Circle, B207 Medium Oval, B228 Small Orchard Tree, and B253 Leaf Stem

Hot press watercolor paper

Cardstock: Memory Box—Vanilla Bean

Note card: Memory Box—Jack O Lantern

Watercolor paints: Winsor & Newton Cotman—Lemon Yellow Hue, Cobalt Blue, and Sap Green

Ink: Tsukineko—VersaMagic Key Lime, Tea Leaves, Jumbo Java, and VersaColor Celadon

Watercolor brush

HOW TO:
Wet a 2" x 3" area of watercolor paper with water, allow it to set for a minute, and then repeat. Load a brush with Lemon Yellow Hue paint and, with the paper laid out horizontally, paint three or four horizontal bands of color across the wet areas. Rinse the brush and apply more water horizontally across the wet area. Load a brush with Cobalt Blue and paint one or two horizontal bands across the bottom of the rectangle, slightly overlapping any yellow that may be there. Rinse and apply more water over the whole area. Allow to rest for a minute or two. Rinse the brush and load with Sap Green, applying the paint sparingly in horizontal strokes near the bottom of the image. If the yellow has become too weak near the top, apply more yellow in horizontal strokes. Rinse the brush and apply more water over the whole area. Let dry completely.

Referring to the photo on page 37, stamp a circle in Key Lime, a circle in Tea Leaves, and the oval in Celadon. Stamp the tree and leaf images over the shapes in Jumbo Java. Trim, layer, and mount the papers to the card.

Page 38   Harvest Leaf
MATERIALS
Stamps: Memory Box—CS 104 Bold Leaf Cling Set

Cold press watercolor paper

Cardstock: Memory Box—Sweet Corn

Note card: Memory Box—Mango

Patterned paper: Rubber Soul—8" x 8" Garden Variety Collection

Watercolor paints: Winsor & Newton Cotman—Cadmium Yellow Pale, Cadmium Orange, and Cadmium Red Pale Hue

Fine-grit sandpaper

Brads

5" length of 3/8"-wide yellow satin ribbon

Needle tool

Watercolor brush

HOW TO:
Load a brush with a thick mixture of Cadmium Yellow Pale paint and brush over the surface of the leaf stamp. Rinse the brush and load with Cadmium Orange paint. Apply orange along all the edges of the stamp. Rinse the brush and load with Cadmium Red Pale. Apply small amounts to the lower area of the leaf and randomly toward the top of the

leaf. Stamp the image onto watercolor paper. While the paint is still wet, rinse the brush and apply plain water to the painted areas, staying within the painted boundaries. Work the painted area slightly to raise the paint up off the surface, and then move to a new area. When the entire image has been wetted with plain water, evaluate to see if the leaf is blended enough. You may repeat adding water to the image, which will smooth out the dark and light areas and make them less distinct. Let dry and trim to size. Cut a rectangle of Sweet Corn cardstock ⅜" longer and wider than the watercolor paper.

Sand the edges of the Mango note card and the Sweet Corn rectangle. Secure the ribbon between the watercolor image and the Sweet Corn rectangle. Mount the layered materials to the card. Fold the ends of the ribbon under and poke through the ribbon and the card with a needle tool. Install brads through the holes. Mount a strip of patterned paper across the bottom of the card.

Page 38 Falling Leaves
MATERIALS
Stamps: Memory Box–B252 Leaf Shape and B253 Leaf Stem

Cold press watercolor paper

Cardstock: Memory Box–Mango

Note card: Rubber Soul–Maize

Watercolor paints: Winsor & Newton Cotman–Cadmium Orange, Sap Green, and Cadmium Yellow Pale

Ink: Tsukineko–VersaMagic Jumbo Java

Watercolor brush

HOW TO:
Wet a 1½" x 6" strip of watercolor paper with plain water. Let rest and reapply water. Paint a wash of color over the wet area with Cadmium Orange and add more water over the entire area. Mix Cadmium Orange and Sap Green to create a brown shade, and add that to the wet area on the paper. Apply water over the entire area again, and then let dry completely. Apply a thick mixture (less water, more paint) of Cadmium Yellow Pale to the rubber image on the leaf-shape stamp. Rinse the brush and load with Cadmium Orange. Add a few short strokes of orange onto the yellow area on the rubber, slightly swirling the orange into the yellow areas, but leaving some yellow areas untouched. Stamp the image onto the watercolor paper. Rinse the brush (do not rinse the

stamp) and apply yellow paint to the rubber stamp. Add orange to the stamp, then rinse the brush and add a tiny amount of green along one edge of the stamp. The rubber should have distinct areas of yellow, orange, and green and be just starting to mix together. Stamp the leaf shape onto watercolor paper. Repeat the preceding steps to stamp two more leaves, changing your placement of color on the stamp. Let dry. Stamp the stems with Jumbo Java over the leaf shapes. Cut the watercolor paper to size and mount onto Mango cardstock. Trim ⅛" from the edges of the watercolor paper and mount the strip to the card.

Page 39 Feel Better Soon
MATERIALS
Stamps: Memory Box–D459 Wide Leaf Shape, C460 Wide Leaf Stem, and B661 Feel Better Soon

Cold press watercolor paper

Note card: Memory Box–Peapod

Watercolor paints: Winsor & Newton Cotman–Yellow Ochre, Cerulean Blue, Sap Green, Cadmium Yellow Pale, and Cadmium Red Pale Hue

Ink: Tsukineko–VersaMagic Hint of Pesto

Extra-fine-mist spritzer bottle (filled with water): JudiKins

Watercolor brush

HOW TO:
Create a background wash by painting a 2" x 3" area of watercolor paper with plain water. Let the area rest a minute and repeat. Load a brush with Yellow Ochre and fill the wet area, allowing some areas to remain stronger in color and other areas to become weaker. Rinse the brush and load with Cerulean Blue paint. Add the blue randomly in small lines along the edges of the yellow area. Rinse the brush and add more Yellow Ochre over the wet areas. Rinse the brush and load with Sap Green paint, adding green randomly in gently swirling motions to different parts of the wet area. Allow to rest for a minute or two to watch how the color settles. To achieve a smoother look, add another layer of water, staying inside the boundaries of the original 2" by 3" space so that the edges retain a crisp look. Allow the paper to dry completely before proceeding with stamping.

Load a brush with a thick mixture of Cadmium Yellow Pale paint and apply to the rubber image of the wide leaf shape. Rinse the brush and load with Cadmium Red Pale Hue paint, applying color to the bottom edges of the leaf. Rinse the brush and load with Sap Green, applying the color to the upper half of the leaf.

Mix the green into the yellow area and swirl down into the red area. Holding the bottle about 6" from the stamp, spray a mist of water above the stamp, allowing the mist to drift down onto the rubber. Repeat as necessary to allow the paint to blend on the stamp (but not too much, as you don't want paint dripping off the edges). Stamp the leaf in the center of the watercolor paper. Let dry completely and then stamp the leaf stem with Hint of Pesto. Cut the watercolor paper to size and mount to the card. Stamp "feel better soon" onto the card.

Page 40 Thank You Bouquet
MATERIALS
Stamps: Memory Box–CS-103 Scribble Flower Set and A445 Thank You Light

Cold press watercolor paper

Cardstock: Memory Box–Endive

Note card: Memory Box–Moss

Watercolor markers: Marvy Le Plume II–94 Scarlet, 9 Pink, 43 Brilliant Yellow, 52 Yellow Green, and 96 Jungle Green

Ink: Tsukineko–VersaFine Onyx Black; Impress–Fresh Ink Fig

Watercolor brush

HOW TO:
Stamp the flowers with black ink onto watercolor paper and let dry completely. Using the fine-tipped end of the Scarlet marker, color the tips of the petals just inside the image. Switch to the Pink marker and use the broader tip to add an area of color that follows the contour of the petal. Randomly leave sections of the petals uncolored so that each flower looks unique. With a wet brush and a palette of Brilliant Yellow ink, lift yellow with the brush and paint over the petals, working the Pink and Scarlet areas so that they dissolve and blend into the yellow. Rinse the brush and add plain water to the petal areas, further softening the lines between dark and light colors. Let dry completely. Color with the broad end of the Yellow Green marker around the outside of the flowers but only where they are close to each other. Add some Jungle Green (using the fine-tipped end) between some of the petals. With a wet paintbrush, pull the greens into the open space between the flowers and blend together. Rinse the brush and add plain water to the green area, pulling the coloring between the flowers until it begins to fade. Color a small patch of Pink inside the centers of the flowers, just along the edge of the circular centers.

With a clean, wet brush, dissolve the Pink to fill the entire center. With any leftover color on the brush, randomly add a light layer of Pink to the tips of the petals. Stamp "thank you" with Fig ink onto watercolor paper. Trim, layer, and mount the papers to the card.

Page 40   Rose Invitation
MATERIALS
Stamps: Memory Box—CS-103 Scribble Flower Set

Cold press watercolor paper

Cardstock: Memory Box—Cherry Blossom

Patterned paper: Memory Box—6" x 6" Sugar Collection

Watercolor markers: Marvy Le Plume II—9 Pink, 94 Scarlet, 52 Yellow Green, and 96 Jungle Green

Ink: Tsukineko—VersaFine Onyx Black

8" length of ⅞"-wide pink wired ribbon

⅛" hole punch

Watercolor brush

HOW TO:
Stamp the rose onto the watercolor paper with black ink and let dry completely. On a scrap piece of paper, color an area about 1" square of each color of marker to make a palette. With a clean, damp brush, lift color from the Pink square by rubbing it with the brush and paint a light layer over the rose petals, keeping the brush on the paper constantly. If the brush runs out of color, move the brush to the center and lift off the paper. Get more ink from the Pink square, begin in the center, and finish filling in the rose petals. Rinse the brush and lift color from the Scarlet square, applying it to the center of each rose and shading around each petal. Each petal should remain light at the outer edge and get darker as you approach the center of the flower. To smooth out any lines that may develop, rinse the brush and dry it until it is only slightly damp. Rub over any hard lines of color in a gentle, swirling motion until color is smoothed out. Rinse the brush and lift ink from the Yellow Green square. Paint a light layer of color around the rose images. Rinse the brush and lift color from the Jungle Green square, then paint right around the outside of the roses. Rinse the brush, dry until slightly damp, and then smooth any green lines that haven't blended into the lighter green colors. Layer and adhere the Cherry Blossom cardstock and patterned paper to the watercolor paper. Trim to size and mount onto another piece of Cherry Blossom cardstock. Trim to size, leaving a border around all sides. Punch two holes near the top and tie the ribbon through the holes.

Page 41
Floating Blooms
MATERIALS
Stamps: Memory Box—CS-103 Scribble Flower Set

Cold press watercolor paper

Note card: Rubber Soul—Wave

Watercolor markers: Marvy Le Plume II—53 Pale Blue, 100 Sapphire, 99 Periwinkle, 43 Brilliant Yellow, and 83 Butterscotch

Ink: Tsukineko—VersaFine Onyx Black

Watercolor brush

HOW TO:
Stamp the flowers onto watercolor paper with black ink and let dry. On a scrap piece of paper, color an area about 1" square of each color of marker to make a palette. Begin by lifting the lightest color (Pale Blue) with the brush and painting a light layer of blue over each petal. While the petals are still wet, add more paint along the edges of the petals, at different spots on different petals. Lift Sapphire and paint at the tips and edges of the petals, changing the intensity and position of the color so that no two petals are identical. Finally add Periwinkle at the tips and edges of the petals, again altering the positions where the color is applied to make each petal unique. Rinse the brush and dry it until only slightly damp. Smooth over the entire area of each petal, beginning near the center of the flower and working to the tip in a gentle back-and-forth, swirling motion until the blue inks have all blended. Let dry completely. Lift ink from the Brilliant Yellow square and paint the centers of the flowers. Rinse the brush and lift color from the Butterscotch area of your palette, using it to add shading halfway around the center of the flower over the yellow area. Cut watercolor paper to size and mount to the card.

Page 42   Old-Fashioned Roses
MATERIALS
Stamp: Impress—2053F Rose Branch

Cold press watercolor paper

Cardstock: Memory Box—Sugar Plum

Note card: Memory Box—Currant

Watercolor markers: Marvy Le Plume II—43 Brilliant Yellow, 52 Yellow Green, 96 Jungle Green, and 78 Orchid

Extra-fine-mist spritzer bottle (filled with water): JudiKins

Watercolor brush

HOW TO:
Color the flowers with the Orchid marker. Apply Brilliant Yellow randomly to different areas of the branches on the rubber stamp. Next add Yellow Green, filling most of the branches. Add Jungle Green randomly over the branches, mainly hitting the edges of the rubber (the sides of the leaves and branches). Color the flowers with the Orchid marker. Holding the stamp rubber side up with one hand, mist the stamp with the spritzer bottle and then press the stamp onto the watercolor paper (first stamping). Hold the stamp rubber side up again and spritz again, letting the mist settle onto the rubber. Press the stamp onto a second sheet of watercolor paper (second stamping). Decide which stamping, first or second, works best for the project and trim to size. Mount at an angle onto a similar-sized piece of Sugar Plum cardstock, and then mount to the card.

Page 42
Fiery Flower
MATERIALS
Stamps: Memory Box—D449 Leafy Stem and B433 Looped Flower

Cold press watercolor paper

Cardstock: Memory Box—Sherbet

Patterned paper: Memory Box—6" x 6" Beach Collection

Note card: Memory Box—Red Pepper

Watercolor markers: Marvy Le Plume II—43 Brilliant Yellow, 83 Butterscotch, 9 Pink, and 96 Jungle Green

Extra-fine-mist spritzer bottle (filled with water): JudiKins

Watercolor brush

HOW TO:
Draw a 1" x 4" rectangle onto watercolor paper with the broad tip of a Brilliant Yellow marker. Using the broad tip of the Butterscotch marker, add a little bit of ink to the corners of the yellow rectangle. Color the entire rubber surface of the looped flower with Brilliant Yellow. Switch to the Pink marker and add a few dots randomly over the rubber flower. With the Butterscotch marker, trace the edge of the flower, adding just a small amount of color. Spritz the stamp with water and stamp the flower inside the rectangle, leaving enough space below for the stem. Ink the stem on the rubber stamp with Jungle Green and stamp below the flower. With a clean, wet brush, pull the color from the rectangle line toward the flower without touching the flower or stem. Cut

the watercolor piece to size and mount onto Sherbet cardstock. Trim 1/16" from the edges of the watercolor paper. Cut a scant 3/8" strip of patterned paper and mount to the note card, trimming to size. Mount the stamped flower to the card.

Page 43 Gently Falling Petals
MATERIALS

Stamp: Memory Box—C223 Large Vintage Flower

Cold press watercolor paper

Cardstock: Memory Box—Blue Poppy and Water; Bazzill—Splash

Note card: Memory Box—Water

Buttonhole punch: Punch Bunch

Watercolor markers: Marvy Le Plume II—53 Pale Blue, 100 Sapphire, and 99 Periwinkle

Extra-fine-mist spritzer bottle (filled with water): JudiKins

Watercolor brush

HOW TO:

Apply all three blue colors to the edges of the flower stamp, leaving the middle uncolored except for the very center. Spritz with water and stamp onto watercolor paper. Without cleaning the stamp, reapply the blue colors, adding more or less color to different parts of the stamp edges and in the center, but leaving the majority of the petals uncolored. Spritz and stamp again. Repeat to stamp a total of five images. Trim the paper to size and mount onto Blue Poppy cardstock. Trim 1/16" from the edges of the watercolor paper and mount onto the Water note card. Add a strip of Water cardstock with a torn edge to a piece of watercolor paper and trim to fit on the left side of the card, allowing 1/16" of space on all sides. Mount onto the left side of the card. Punch five buttonhole shapes out of Splash cardstock and glue to the card.

Page 44 Boxed Presents
MATERIALS

Stamps: Memory Box—B286 Small Gift and B473 1" Square

Cardstock: White

Note card: Memory Box—Cranberry

Watercolor pencils: Faber-Castell Albrecht Durer—109 Dark Chrome Yellow, 115 Dark Cadmium Orange, 125 Middle Purple Pink, and 219 Deep Scarlet Red

Ink: Tsukineko—Brilliance Graphite Black, Rocket Red Gold and Sunflower Yellow, and VersaMagic Red Magic and Mango Madness

Watercolor brush

HOW TO:

Ink the edges of the square stamp using a single ink color or combinations of any of the colors. To minimize mixing the ink on the pads, ink the image with lighter colors first and darker colors last. Stamp nine squares onto white cardstock. Stamp the small gift with black ink in the middle of each square and let dry completely. Color in the gift with different colored pencils, slightly overlapping colors. With a slightly wet brush, blend colors together in one pass, taking care not to get the paper too wet. Let dry completely. Color around the outside of the gift image if desired to fill in a little more color and wet sparingly, so as not to curl the paper. Cut the squares out and mount to the card.

Page 44 Just Married
MATERIALS

Stamps: Memory Box—C593 Hill and B669 Car & Heart

Cardstock: White; Memory Box—Currant

Note card: Memory Box—Cherry Blossom

Watercolor pencils: Faber-Castell Albrecht Durer—142 Madder, 126 Permanent Carmine, and 140 Light Ultramarine

Ink: Tsukineko—VersaFine Onyx Black and VersaMagic Tea Leaves and Orchid

Self-stick note

Sponge dauber

White dimensional paint

Watercolor brush

HOW TO:

Stamp the hill onto white cardstock with Tea Leaves. Stamp the car and heart in black onto white cardstock and let dry completely. Shade the car in with the Madder pencil, coloring heavily at the front and back ends of the car and lightening the pressure in the middle. Color the heart a solid layer of Permanent Carmine. With a damp brush, rub over the car to dissolve the color, being careful not to get the paper too wet. Wet the heart in the same way. Working from the tip of the Light Ultramarine pencil, get a small amount of blue paint onto the brush and trace along the edges of the car's windows. Create a stencil

by cutting cloud shapes from a self-stick note, and use a dauber to apply Orchid ink over the stencil to create cloud lines. Trim, layer, and mount the papers to the card. Add dots of dimensional paint behind the car.

Page 44 Thank You, Thank You Very Much
MATERIALS

Stamps: Memory Box—SS-103 Handpicked Flower Set

Cardstock: White; Memory Box—Key Lime and Granny Smith

Watercolor pencils: Faber-Castell Albrecht Durer—205 Cadmium Yellow Lemon, 107 Cadmium Yellow, 171 Light Green, and 108 Dark Cadmium Yellow

Ink: Tsukineko—Brilliance Graphite Black

Computer and color printer

Sewing machine and lime green thread

Font: 2Peas Mademoiselle

Leaf punch: EK Success

Watercolor brush

HOW TO:

Print "thank you" onto white cardstock and stamp flower images with black ink around the words, masking the words as necessary. Let dry completely. Working with a brush, rub the tip of a Cadmium Yellow Lemon pencil and add a light layer to all the flower petals. Rub the tip of a Light Green pencil with a wet brush and apply paint to the tips of each petal. Let dry completely. With a slightly damp brush, blend the green and yellow areas briefly until smooth, cleaning the brush between each petal. Once the petals are dry, apply Cadmium Yellow to the centers of each flower, working with a brush from the tip of the pencil. Switch to Dark Cadmium Yellow and shade one side of each flower center. Let dry completely. Trim, layer, and mount the top two paper layers. Sew a wavy line along the top of the layered papers, and then mount to the card. Punch out Key Lime leaves, fold slightly, and glue to the card.

Page 45 Keep Me in Stitches
MATERIALS

Stamp: Hero Arts—F3777 Stitched Posy

Hot press watercolor paper

Patterned paper: Memory Box—6" x 6" Beach Collection

Note card: Memory Box—Russian Sage

Watercolor pencils: Faber-Castell Albrecht Durer—156 Cobalt Green, 140 Light Ultramarine, 110 Phthalo Blue, 171 Light Green, and 107 Cadmium Yellow

Ink: Tsukineko—VersaFine Onyx Black

Watercolor brush

HOW TO:

Stamp the flower image with black ink onto watercolor paper. Apply Cobalt Green, Light Ultramarine, Phthalo Blue, and Light Green around the flower image. Fade the pencil as you color further away from the flower image. With a wet brush, begin blending around the flower, massaging the color around the paper in a gentle figure-eight motion. Keep the brush on the paper at all times except when more water is needed. To get more water, move the brush to the edge of the watercolor piece and lift. Add more water to the brush (rinsing off color if necessary) and begin where the brush was lifted from the paper. Once the color has all dissolved around the flower, let it set a minute. If the background requires more blending, load the brush with water and work the background again, painting over the whole area with plain water. Let dry completely. Rinse the brush and rub the tip of the Cadmium Yellow pencil until yellow paint is on the brush. Use it to fill in the center of the flower. Tear the edges of the watercolor piece and mount onto patterned paper. Trim the patterned paper to size and mount to the card.

Page 45 Swirling Rainbows

MATERIALS

Stamp: Hero Arts—H3049 Fancy Swirls

Cold press watercolor paper

Cardstock: Rubber Soul—Periwinkle and Hydrangea

Note card: Memory Box—Russian Sage

Watercolor pencils: Faber-Castell Albrecht Durer—205 Cadmium Yellow Lemon, 104 Light Yellow Glaze, 107 Cadmium Yellow, 109 Dark Chrome Yellow, 115 Dark Cadmium Orange, 125 Middle Purple Pink, 219 Deep Scarlet Red, 129 Pink Madder Lake, 136 Purple Violet, 110 Phthalo Blue, and 140 Light Ultramarine

Ink: Tsukineko—VersaFine Onyx Black

Watercolor brush

HOW TO:

Stamp fancy swirls with black ink onto watercolor paper and let dry completely. Match up pencils in analogous groups:

> Cadmium Yellow Lemon, Light Yellow Glaze, and Cadmium Yellow
>
> Dark Chrome Yellow and Dark Cadmium Orange
>
> Middle Purple Pink, Deep Scarlet Red, and Pink Madder Lake
>
> Purple Violet, Phthalo Blue, and Light Ultramarine

Begin shading at the center of a swirl with Cadmium Yellow Lemon and fade out quickly. Add Light Yellow Glaze further along the path of a swirl, overlapping the first color. Add Cadmium Yellow next to the second color, overlapping slightly. With a wet brush, work the first color into the second and continue to the third until all colors are blended together. Skip to another section of the design so that colors don't bleed into each other, and repeat the process using any of the analogous color groups listed above until the entire image is filled. Place complementary color schemes next to each other for high contrast (see "Blending" on page 7). Allow the watercolor piece to dry and then trim, layer, and mount the papers to the card.

Page 46 Garden of Flowers

MATERIALS

Stamp: Memory Box—C704 Stem Flower

Cold press watercolor paper

Cardstock: Memory Box—Cherry Blossom

Note card: Memory Box—Cotton Candy

Watercolor pencils: Faber-Castell Albrecht Durer—129 Pink Madder Lake and 171 Light Green

Ink: Tsukineko—VersaFine Vintage Sepia

Pink rickrack trim

Watercolor brush

HOW TO:

Stamp the flower image four times with Vintage Sepia along the bottom edge of the watercolor paper and let dry completely. Shade the base of the petals with Pink Madder Lake and wet with a brush, pulling the color up to the tips of the petals. Rub the tip of the Light Green pencil with a wet brush and paint over the stems and leaves. Trim, layer, and mount

the papers to the card. Cut bits of rickrack to create tiny photo corners and glue around the corners of the watercolor paper.

Page 46 Thinking of You
MATERIALS

Stamp: Impress—2051D Small Peony

Cold press watercolor paper

Note card: Memory Box—Cherry Blossom

Watercolor pencil: Faber-Castell Albrecht Durer—129 Pink Madder Lake

Ink: Tsukineko—VersaFine Vintage Sepia

Watercolor brush

HOW TO:

Stamp three images along the edge of the watercolor paper with Vintage Sepia and let dry. Color the centers of the flower images with Pink Madder Lake pencil. With a clean, wet brush, work the center of the flowers and pull the color to the tips of the petals. Let dry completely. Tear down the center of the note card, exposing the white beneath the printed color on the front of the card. Cut the stamped watercolor paper to the size of the note card. Mount the watercolor piece inside the card.

Page 47 Peony in Bloom
MATERIALS

Stamp: Impress—2052F Large Double Peony

Hot press watercolor paper

Cardstock: White; Memory Box—Cherry Blossom

Note card: Memory Box—Cotton Candy

Watercolor pencil: Faber-Castell Albrecht Durer—129 Pink Madder Lake

Ink: Tsukineko—VersaFine Onyx Black and VersaMagic Pixie Dust

Scallop tag punch: Marvy LVSJCP

Sponge dauber

Computer and printer

Font: 2Peas Mademoiselle

9" length of ⅛"-wide sage green satin ribbon

3 pink ⅛" eyelets

Watercolor brush

HOW TO:

Stamp the image with black ink onto watercolor paper and let dry completely. Apply one layer of plain water over the entire flower image and let it rest a minute. Rub the tip of the Pink Madder Lake pencil with a wet brush to pick up some paint and apply to the inner folds and tips of the flower petals. Rinse the brush and apply plain water to the open space of the petals, pulling color from the tips of the petals toward the center. Allow the paper to dry completely. Print messages on the white cardstock and punch out with the scallop tag punch. Rub the edges of the tags with Pixie Dust ink. Mount the watercolor piece onto Cherry Blossom cardstock. Trim 1/8" from the edges of the watercolor paper and mount onto the note card. Add ribbon to the tags and mount to the card.

Page 49
Vintage Love Note
MATERIALS
Stamps: Memory Box—E453 Script Block and C188 Needlepoint Heart

Cardstock: Memory Box—Cotton Candy and Cherry Blossom

Note card: Memory Box—Currant

Watercolor paints: Twinkling H2Os—Passion, Playful Peony, and Pink Azalea

Ink: Tsukineko—VersaColor Opera Pink

Extra-fine-mist spritzer bottle (filled with water): JudiKins

HOW TO:
Stamp the script block image with Opera Pink onto Cotton Candy cardstock. Paint the needlepoint heart on the stamp with a thick layer of the three paint colors and let dry. Hold the spray bottle about 6" above the heart stamp, rubber side up. Spray so that a fine mist settles onto the rubber of the stamp and rewets the paint. Stamp the heart over the script block. Trim, layer, and mount the papers to the card.

Page 50
Gerber Daisies
MATERIALS
Stamp: Memory Box—A826 Big Bumblebee

Cardstock: Memory Box—Meadow, Licorice, and Cranberry

Note card: Memory Box—Granny Smith

Colored pencils: Prismacolor—(wings) 1087 Powder Blue; (body) 916 Canary Yellow and 1002 Yellowed Orange

Ink: Tsukineko—Brilliance Graphite Black

Balloon punch tool: Marvy

Petal punch tool: Carla Craft

White shrink plastic

Fine-grit sandpaper

HOW TO:
Sand shrink plastic and stamp bumblebees onto shrink plastic with black ink. Once dry, color in the bumblebees, cut them out, and shrink, following the manufacturer's directions. Cut the Meadow cardstock to the size of the note card. Cut two stem shapes out of the Meadow cardstock and mount the Meadow piece onto the Granny Smith note card. Punch the balloon out of the Licorice cardstock and glue to the top of the stems. Punch the petals out of Cranberry cardstock and glue over the balloons. Glue the bumblebees to the card.

Page 50 Snowy Globe
MATERIALS
Stamp: Memory Box—D715 Carved Snowglobe

White cardstock

Note card: Memory Box—Crimson

Colored pencils: Prismacolor—937 Tuscan Red, 924 Crimson Red, 923 Scarlet Lake, 916 Canary Yellow, 1087 Powder Blue, 1024 Blue Slate, and 1005 Limepeel

Ink: Tsukineko—VersaFine Onyx Black

2 leaf embellishments

HOW TO:
Stamp the image with black ink onto white cardstock. Color in the background starting with Tuscan Red, and then Crimson Red and Scarlet Lake, blending toward the middle. Leave a scant amount of space around the snow globe. Draw a Canary Yellow line around the globe, in the uncolored space, to create a glow. Partially color the sky in Powder Blue and the bottom of the snowy hill in Blue Slate, leaving much of the sky and hill uncolored. Color the vine and leaves with Limepeel. Trim the image to size, mount onto the note card, and add leaf embellishments.

Page 51
Autumnal Dress
MATERIALS
Stamp: Lockhart Designs—2011 Acorn and Fall Leaves Vegetable Couture Dress

Patterned paper: Memory Box—6" × 6" Homespun Collection

Note card: Memory Box—Cantaloupe

Colored pencils: Prismacolor—(dress) 1012 Jasmine, 989 Chartreuse, 917 Sunburst Yellow, 1032 Pumpkin Orange, 923 Scarlet Lake, 944 Terra Cotta, and 937 Tuscan Red; (acorn) 1095 Black Raspberry and 943 Burnt Ochre; (hanger) 1098 Artichoke

Ink: Tsukineko—VersaFine Onyx Black

8" length of 7/8"-wide orange ribbon

Sewing machine and white thread

HOW TO:
Stamp the dress image with black ink onto patterned paper. Color in the leaves of the dress, beginning at the edge of each leaf with deep colors and blending to lighter shades in the center. Draw over the leaf veins with Chartreuse. Color the acorn and hanger. Trim the paper to size and mount to the card. Ruche the ribbon on the sewing machine and glue along the edge of the patterned paper.

Page 51 Knit and Purl
MATERIALS
Stamp: Lockhart Designs—2031 Basket of Yarn

Cardstock: Memory Box—Sherbet, Cantaloupe, and Persimmon

Note card: Memory Box—Eggshell

Colored pencils: Prismacolor—1024 Blue Slate, 1001 Salmon, 926 Carmine Red, 918 Orange, 917 Sunburst Yellow, 942 Yellow Ochre, 943 Burnt Ochre, 944 Terra Cotta, 1012 Jasmine, and 914 Cream

Ink: Tsukineko—VersaFine Onyx Black

HOW TO:
Cut 17 strips about 1/4" × 2" from the Sherbet, Cantaloupe, and Persimmon cardstock. Glue the strips to the bottom of the card, allowing 1/4" to hang over the bottom. Let dry and then trim the bottom even with the edge of the card. Stamp the basket image with black ink onto the Eggshell card. Use Blue Slate on the knitting needles and various shades of yellows, oranges, and red over the balls of yarn. Use Cream to help blend the yellows and oranges. Blend the Terra Cotta, Orange, and Jasmine pencils across each basket weave. Blend left to right or from the edges to the center on the horizontal regions, and vary the blending in the vertical regions.

Page 52 Cherry Blossoms

MATERIALS

Stamps: Memory Box–B103 Medium Allium, D448 Painted Stem, AA440 Leaf (tiny), A362 Heart Petals, and AA221 Small Vintage Flower

Note card: Memory Box–Eggshell

Ink: Tsukineko–VersaColor Opera Pink (Small Vintage Flower) and Orchid (Heart Petals and Medium Allium), and VersaMagic Jumbo Java (Painted Stem) and Tea Leaves (Leaf)

HOW TO:

Stamp the stem with Jumbo Java, connecting the stems to form branches. Stamp the allium and the heart petal images with Orchid at the tips of the stems. Stamp the small flower in the centers of the alliums with Opera Pink. Fill in along the branches with the tiny leaf stamp in Tea Leaves.

Page 52 A Tiny Part of Something Bigger

MATERIALS

Stamps: Memory Box–B248 Small Triangle, B249 Short Pine, B254 Wide Triangle, C246 Tall Triangle, C206 Mega Oval, B207 Medium Oval, D210 1¾" Circle, B229 ¾" Circle, D211 Orchard Tree, B228 Small Orchard Tree, C247 Tall Pine, B255 Wide Pine, C208 Small Border Tree, E209 Large Border Tree, and A136 Birdie

Note card: Memory Box–Eggshell

Colored pencil: Prismacolor–923 Scarlet Lake

Ink: Tsukineko–VersaColor Celadon (shapes) and Pinecone (trees), VersaMagic Tea Leaves (shapes), and VersaFine Onyx Black

HOW TO:

Stamp half of the shapes with Celadon, spacing them around the card. Stamp the other half of the shapes with Tea Leaves, working around the Celadon shapes. Stamp the trees with Pinecone, centering them onto the triangle, circle, and oval images. Stamp the birdie with black ink and color it in with a solid layer of Scarlet Lake.

Page 53 Zen Garden

MATERIALS

Stamps: Memory Box–C219 Solid Marigold, C226 Large Flat Leaf, C266 Leaf Pick, AA197 Solid Fleur, AA439 Forget Me Not, B261 Leaf Swirl, B252 Leaf Shape, B253 Leaf Stem, AA440 Leaf (tiny), and AA221 Small Vintage Flower

Cardstock: Memory Box–Endive

Note card: Memory Box–Eggshell

Ink: Tsukineko–VersaMagic Sugar Cane (Leaf Shape), Tea Leaves (Leaf Swirl), and Red Magic (Solid Marigold, Small Vintage Flower, and Solid Fleur), and VersaColor Pinecone (Leaf Stem) and Polar Blue Forget-Me-Not; ColorBox–Moss Green (Leaf Pick, Leaf, and Large Flat Leaf)

HOW TO:

Stamp the marigolds onto the note card first in Red Magic ink, leaving a lot of space around them to fill in with leaves. Stamp the various leaves onto the card, making sure that similar leaves are spread out across the card. Fill in the remaining area with smaller flower images, making sure to distribute them evenly across the space. Cut a strip of Endive cardstock and mount to the edge of the note card along the fold.

Page 53 Sketched Branches

MATERIALS

Stamps: Memory Box–B252 Leaf Shape and B222 Medium Vintage Flower

Note card: Memory Box–Eggshell

Colored pencil: Prismacolor–946 Dark Brown

Ink: ColorBox–Moss Green (Leaf Shape); Tsukineko–VersaColor Opera Pink (Medium Vintage Flower)

HOW TO:

Draw quick strokes of color across the card, using the Dark Brown pencil. Stamp the leaves with Moss Green ink and then stamp the flowers with Opera Pink.

Page 54 Snowy Winter Tree

MATERIALS

Stamp: Savvy Stamps–868G Leaf Tree

Cardstock: White; Memory Box–Blueberry

Patterned paper: Memory Box–6" x 6" Winter Wonderland Collection

Note card: Memory Box–Blue Poppy

Colored pencils: Prismacolor–1101 Denim Blue, 904 Cerulean Blue, and 1087 Powder Blue

Ink: Tsukineko–VersaMagic Night Sky

Star sequin

HOW TO:

Stamp the tree image with Night Sky ink onto white cardstock. Color each leaf with the blue pencils, blending from dark to light from the base to the tip of each leaf. Trim to size and mount onto Blueberry cardstock. Mount onto two additional layers of cardstock to build depth, and then trim 1/16" from the edges. Cut the patterned paper into wavy strips and mount to the card, trimming the edges even with the edges of the card. Mount the tree image to the card. Glue the star sequin to the tree.

Page 55 Blooming Pot of Tulips

MATERIALS

Stamp: Lockhart Stamp Company– 2025 Tulips

White cardstock

Note card: Memory Box–Blue Poppy

Colored pencils: Prismacolor–(flowers and outer border) 916 Canary Yellow, 1002 Yellowed Orange, 918 Orange, 929 Pink, 994 Process Red, 930 Magenta, 956 Lilac, 993 Hot Pink, 926 Carmine Red, and 934 Lavender; (leaves) 989 Chartreuse, 913 Spring Green, and 1005 Limepeel; (background) 1087 Powder Blue, 1011 Denim Blue, and 992 Light Aqua; (flowerpot) 929 Pink, 994 Process Red, 918 Orange, and 934 Lavender

Ink: Tsukineko–VersaFine Onyx Black

HOW TO:

Stamp the tulip image with black ink onto the white cardstock. Color in the flowers, shading from the bottom to the top of each petal. Color in the blue background areas, blending from dark to light toward the center. Color in the border with short lengths of color. Color the leaves in green, blending from the base of each leaf to the tip. Color the flower pot. Cut out and mount to the card.

Page 56 Put Your Love on the Line

MATERIALS

Stamp: Memory Box–A372 Love Tag

Note card: Memory Box–Eggshell

Ink: Tsukineko–VersaMagic Perfect Plumeria and VersaColor Orchid and Opera Pink

Sewing machine and pink thread

HOW TO:

Sew thread in a curved arc across the card. Stamp the love tag along the sewn line in consecutive colors, from light to dark, repeating along the entire length of the line.

Page 56   Easter Chick

MATERIALS

Stamps: Savvy Stamps—812C Happy Easter to You, 414G Floral Background, and 810B Chick with Bunny Ears

Hot press watercolor paper

Cardstock: Memory Box—Endive

Note card: Memory Box—Cotton Candy

Colored pencils: Prismacolor—916 Canary Yellow, 914 Cream, 1018 Pink Rose, and 918 Orange

Ink: Tsukineko—VersaMagic Pixie Dust and VersaFine Onyx Black; Impress—Fresh Ink Pink Lemonade

HOW TO:

Stamp the floral background with Pixie Dust onto watercolor paper. Stamp the chick with black ink onto a scrap piece of watercolor paper and color in with yellow and cream colored pencils, blending from dark to light from the bottom of the chick upward. Outline the hat in Pink Rose and color in the beak with Orange. Cut out the chick's body and hat, leaving the wings and feet. Stamp the chick again with black ink onto the floral background area and mount the chick's body and hat onto the background, aligning the images. Trim, layer, and mount the papers to the card. Stamp "happy easter to you" with Pink Lemonade.

Page 57   Floral Print Invitation

MATERIALS

Stamp: Hero Arts—H3258 Real Dill

Cold press watercolor paper

Cardstock: Memory Box—Meadow

Watercolor paints: Twinkling H2Os—Pink Azalea, Royal Orchid, Gold Dust, Lemon Grass, and Sun Burst

Font: Autumn Leaves Constitution

Extra-fine-mist spritzer bottle (filled with water): JudiKins

Computer and printer

Craft knife

HOW TO:

Apply Pink Azalea, Royal Orchid, and Gold Dust paints to the flower part of the rubber stamp. Paint the stems on the rubber stamp with Lemon Grass paint. Allow the paint to dry on the stamp, then mist with water and press the stamp onto the watercolor paper. Add a few hints of Sun Burst paint onto and around

the flower image. Print the words "an invitation" onto the lower-right side of the Meadow cardstock. Fold the Meadow cardstock in half so the text is horizontal, and then trim the card to size, centering the text across the width of the card. Make a slit, above and below "an invitation", cutting to within ⅛" of the edges to tuck the watercolor piece into. Trim the watercolor image to size and insert into the slits.

Page 58   String of Hearts

MATERIALS

Stamp: Memory Box—B384 Pair of Hearts

Cold press watercolor paper

Cardstock: Memory Box—Sweet Corn, Daffodil, Key Lime, Granny Smith, Blueberry, Hyacinth, Sugar Plum, Currant, Cranberry, Mango, and Licorice

Note card: Memory Box—Cotton Candy

Watercolor pencils: Faber-Castell Albrecht Durer—115 Dark Cadmium Orange, 108 Dark Cadmium Yellow, 107 Cadmium Yellow, 171 Light Green, 168 Earth Green Yellowish, 151 Helioblue-Reddish, 136 Purple Violet, 142 Madder, 124 Rose Carmine, and 109 Dark Chrome Yellow

Ink: Tsukineko—VersaFine Onyx Black

HOW TO:

Stamp the hearts across the watercolor paper. Color the hearts, gradually changing colors as they appear on the color wheel (see "Blending" on page 7). Overlap colors where the images overlap. Wet the image with a brush, allowing overlapping colors to mix together. Let dry completely. Working from the tip of the pencil, add more color to overlapped areas as necessary. Trim the heart design to size and mount onto Licorice cardstock. Trim ¹⁄₁₆" from the edges. Cut squares of similar size from the remaining cardstock and mount them to the card, overlapping the colors and keeping similar shades next to each other. Mount the heart design to the card over the colored squares.

Page 59   Late Fall Evening

MATERIALS

Stamps: Rubber Soul—275K Tree Tile; Memory Box—AA599 Maple Leaf

Hot press watercolor paper

Cardstock: Memory Box—Concord Grape

Note card: Memory Box—Lavender

Watercolor pencils: Faber-Castell Albrecht Durer—249 Mauve, 136 Purple Violet, 120 Ultramarine, and 140 Light Ultramarine

Ink: Tsukineko—VersaMark Clear, VersaColor Heliotrope, and VersaMagic Concord Grape and Pretty Petunia

Clear embossing powder

Iron (wool setting)

Newsprint

Sponge or jumbo sponge dauber

HOW TO:

Stamp the tree tile image onto watercolor paper with clear ink and emboss with clear powder. With a wet brush, pick up paint from the tip of the pencils and paint in the background around the trees. Stamp several leaf images with clear ink onto the Lavender note card and emboss with clear powder. Sponge over the leaves with different shades of purple ink. Put the note card face down onto newsprint and iron the back of the card, removing the embossing powder. Cut out the tree tile image, mount onto Concord Grape cardstock, trim ¹⁄₁₆" from the edges, and mount to the card.

Page 59   Polka-Dot Flower Card

MATERIALS

Stamps: Savvy Stamps—878I Large Medium Dot Background and 453D Hyacinth Trio

Cold press watercolor paper

Cardstock: Memory Box—Moss, Russian Sage, and Endive

Note card: Memory Box—Moss

Watercolor paints: Twinkling H2Os—(flowers) Blue Ice, Majestic Blue, and Royal Orchid; (leaves) Moss Green; (background) Sun Burst and Lemon Grass

Ink: Impress—Fresh Ink Freesia

Extra-fine-mist spritzer bottle (filled with water): JudiKins

Metal frame, Blueberry scrapbook paint, flower brad, and slot punching tool: Making Memories

Computer and printer

Font: Roselyn

Paper flower: Savvy Stamps

HOW TO:

Wet the watercolor paper with water and paint a 1½" x 2" rectangle using Sunburst and Lemon Grass around the outer edges, leaving an open space in the middle. Let dry. Paint the flower and leaf colors directly onto the rubber stamp and let dry. With the stamp rubber side up, mist with water to reactivate the paint and press onto watercolor paper in the center of the painted rectangle. Let dry, and then trim the image to size. Mount onto Moss cardstock and trim 1/16" from the edges of the watercolor paper. Stamp the dot background with Freesia ink onto Russian Sage cardstock and trim to size. Mount onto Endive cardstock and trim 1/16" from the edges. Cut a rectangle of Russian Sage about 1/2" longer and wider than the bordered dot rectangle and punch slots in opposite corners. Mount the paper layers to the card. Paint the metal frame Blueberry. Print out "best wishes" and insert into the frame. Glue the frame and the flower to the card. Install the flower brads.

Page 60
Carved Acorns
MATERIALS
Stamp: Rubbermoon—GE 2657 F Acorn Block

Cardstock: White; Memory Box—Cranberry and Licorice

Note card: Memory Box—Red Pepper

Watercolor paints: Twinkling H2Os—Sky Blue, Teal Zircon, Blue Grass, Pink Azalea, Gold Dust, Solar Gold, Ginger Peach, and Sunburst

Colored pencils: Prismacolor—917 Sunburst Yellow, 944 Terra Cotta, 1032 Pumpkin Orange, and 1034 Goldenrod

Ink: Tsukineko—Brilliance Graphite Black

Red metal tag: 7 Gypsies

Computer and printer

Font: Tennessee

Yellow brad

HOW TO:
Brush various shades of paint onto white cardstock, slightly overlapping colors, and let dry. Stamp the acorn three times onto the painted areas and let dry. Color in the acorns and leaves with pencils. Cut out the acorns, mount onto Cranberry cardstock, and trim to size. Mount the Cranberry cardstock onto Licorice cardstock and trim 1/16" from the edges of the Cranberry. Print "for you" on a computer printer, trim to size, and mount onto the metal tag. Attach the tag to the card with a brad.

Page 60   Floating Flower Stems
MATERIALS
Stamps: Hero Arts—G3827 Sketch Line Rectangle and H2365 Old French Writing

Hot press watercolor paper

Cardstock: Memory Box—Meadow and Cranberry

Note card: Rubber Soul—Maize

Watercolor markers: Marvy Le Plume II—43 Brilliant Yellow, 83 Butterscotch, and 46 Crimson Lake

Watercolor pencils: Faber-Castell Albrecht Durer—184 Dark Naples Ochre and 108 Dark Cadmium Yellow

Ink: Tsukineko—Brilliance Graphite Black

Flower punch: Carla Craft

Lemon yellow liquid pearls: Ranger

Sewing machine and sage green thread

HOW TO:
Ink the French writing image with all shades of watercolor markers and stamp onto the watercolor paper. Stamp the sketch rectangle with black ink over the writing image. Let dry. Color directly on the paper inside the rectangle with the watercolor pencils and blend inside the rectangle with a wet brush, working to dissolve the writing. Once dry, sew lines onto the paper for stems. Punch the flowers from Cranberry cardstock and mount onto the tops of the stems. Add liquid pearls to the centers of the flowers. Trim, layer, and mount the papers to the card.

Page 61
Heartfelt Tag
MATERIALS
Stamp: Memory Box—D377 Vine Heart

Cold press watercolor paper

Patterned paper: Memory Box—6" x 6" Sweetheart Collection

Note card: Memory Box—Cotton Candy

Watercolor pencil: Faber-Castell Albrecht Durer—129 Pink Madder Lake

Ink: Tsukineko—VersaMark Clear

Clear embossing powder

5" length of 3/8"-wide pink twill tape

Sewing machine and pink thread

3/4", 1/2", and 1/8" circle punches

HOW TO:
Stamp the heart image with clear ink onto watercolor paper and emboss with clear embossing powder. With a wet brush, work from the tip of the colored pencil to fill in the image, allowing lighter and darker areas to

develop across the image. Cut a freehand tag shape from patterned paper and mount to a second piece of patterned paper, trimming to create a narrow border. Stitch around the edge of the top tag. Punch a 3/4" and a 1/2" circle and cut a 1/2" x 1 1/4" rectangle from the patterned papers. Layer and mount the rectangle and circles at the top of the tag and punch a 1/8" hole through the center of the circles, through all layers. Insert the twill tape through the hole and glue in place. Mount the heart image to the tag and mount the tag to the card.

Page 62
Birthday Bouquet
MATERIALS
Stamps: Rubber Soul—2511D Flower and 242K Grass Lines; Memory Box—A446 Happy Birthday; Savvy Stamps—8251 Large Dashed Border

Cardstock: Memory Box—Cherry Blossom

Note card: Memory Box—Cotton Candy

Watercolor pencil: Faber-Castell Albrecht Durer—129 Pink Madder Lake

Ink: Tsukineko—VersaColor Orchid and VersaMagic Jumbo Java

Scalloped metal frame: Making Memories

HOW TO:
Stamp the dashed border with Orchid ink onto the note card. Stamp the grass and flowers with Jumbo Java over the dashed border. With a wet brush and working from the tip of the colored pencil, pick up color and apply paint around the centers of the flowers, allowing the color to go outside the lines. Stamp "happy birthday" in Jumbo Java onto Cherry Blossom cardstock and trim to fit behind the metal frame. Mount the framed words to the card.

Page 62   Stitched Heart
MATERIALS
Stamps: Hero Arts—H3780 Large Stitched Heart; Rubber Soul—7061 Love

Cold press watercolor paper

Note card: Memory Box—Cherry Blossom

Watercolor pencils: Faber-Castell Albrecht Durer—125 Middle Purple Pink and 129 Pink Madder Lake

Ink: Tsukineko—Brilliance Graphite Black and VersaColor Opera Pink

Sponge or sponge dauber

7" length of 3/8"-wide brown polka-dot ribbon

HOW TO:

Cut a piece of watercolor paper to the size of the note card. Stamp the heart image onto the watercolor paper with black ink and let dry. Apply watercolor pencils to the inside of the heart and paint with water to dissolve. Sponge half of the background with Opera Pink and stamp the "love" image with black ink over the heart. Tear one edge of the watercolor paper and mount onto the note card. Tear the edge of the card front and glue the ribbon along the folded edge.

Page 63 Tulip Vase
MATERIALS

Stamps: Rubber Soul—2503G Slim Vase and 2505G Tulip; Savvy Stamps—385E Mini Dot Background

Cardstock: Memory Box—Cotton Candy and Cherry Blossom

Note card: Rubber Soul—Sweet Pea Pink

Watercolor pencils: Faber-Castell Albrecht Durer—125 Middle Purple Pink and 129 Pink Madder Lake

Ink: Tsukineko—VersaMagic Jumbo Java and VersaColor Orchid

Sewing machine

7" length of brown rickrack trim

HOW TO:

Trim away half of the note card front, reserving the piece that was cut away. Cut a piece of Cherry Blossom cardstock to the outside dimensions of the note card and mount to the inside back of the card. Glue the rickrack trim to the inside edge of the note card front (flap). Stamp the dot background with Orchid ink onto Cotton Candy cardstock. Stamp the vase and flower with Jumbo Java ink and let dry. With a wet brush and working from the tip of the pencil, paint in the tulip and vase with a blend of the two pink pencils. Trim the image to size and stitch around the edges using a sewing machine without thread to create a border. Mount the image onto the reserved piece of note card, trim to size, and glue to the front flap of the card.

Page 64 Halloween Party Tag
MATERIALS

Stamp: Memory Box—AA338 Tiny Jack O Lantern

Cardstock: Memory Box—Mango, Licorice, Eggshell, and Jack O Lantern

Colored pencils: Prismacolor—916 Canary Yellow and 918 Orange

Ink: Tsukineko—VersaFine Onyx Black

Sewing machine and black thread

Computer and printer

Font: Autumn Leaves Outdoors

¾", ½", and ⅛" circle punches

10" length of ⅜"-wide black satin ribbon

Fine-grit sandpaper

HOW TO:

Print the invitation onto Eggshell cardstock and sew a curved line above the words. Stamp the Tiny Jack O Lantern several times along the thread line and color in with colored pencils. Trim the image to size and mount onto Jack O Lantern cardstock. Trim a scant ⅛" from the edges. Cut a tag shape from Mango cardstock, sand the edges lightly, and mount the layered design onto the tag. Punch a ¾" circle from Licorice cardstock and a ½" circle from Mango cardstock. Layer and mount the circles onto the tag and punch a ⅛" hole in the center of the circles through all layers. Insert the ribbon through the hole and tie.

Page 64 Pumpkin Harvest
MATERIALS

Stamp: Memory Box—D560 Pumpkin Field

Cold press watercolor paper

Cardstock: Memory Box—Sherbet and Gourd

Patterned paper: Memory Box—6" x 6" Spooky Collection

Note card: Memory Box—Mango

Watercolor paints: Twinkling H2Os—(sky) Poppy Red, Deep Coral, Persimmon, and Yellow Rose; (ground) Sunburst, Sunflower, Lemon Grass, and Irish Mist

Watercolor marker: Marvy Le Plume II—83 Butterscotch

Colored pencil: Prismacolor—916 Canary Yellow

Ink: Tsukineko—VersaFine Onyx Black

7" length of ⅞"-wide burnt orange ribbon

HOW TO:

Stamp the pumpkin field onto watercolor paper with black ink. Paint in the sky and ground with watercolor paints and let dry completely. Color in the moon with the Canary Yellow pencil and color the pumpkins with the Butterscotch marker. Trim, layer, and mount the papers and ribbon to the card.

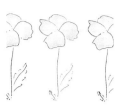

Page 65 Row of Misty Flowers
MATERIALS

Stamp: Memory Box—C697 Dainty Flower

Cardstock: Memory Box—Endive

Patterned paper: Memory Box—6" x 6" Beach Collection

Note card: White

Colored pencils: Prismacolor—1024 Blue Slate and 989 Chartreuse

Ink: Tsukineko—VersaFine Onyx Black and VersaMagic Sea Breeze

Sponge or sponge dauber

HOW TO:

Stamp a row of flowers across the card with black ink. Sponge Sea Breeze ink over the flower heads in each image. Color in the petal tips softly with the Blue Slate pencil and color the leaves softly with the Chartreuse pencil. Cut a strip of Endive cardstock about 1½" wide and a strip of patterned paper 1/16" narrower. Layer and mount the papers along the lower edge of the card front, trimming to size.

Page 66 Flower Patch
MATERIALS

Stamp: Memory Box—C700 Flower Patch

Cardstock: Memory Box—Holly Berry, Key Lime, and Eggshell

Patterned paper: Memory Box—6" x 6" Beach and Homespun Collections

Note card: Memory Box—Cranberry

Colored pencils: Prismacolor—(leaves and stems) 989 Chartreuse and 1005 Limepeel; (flowers) 916 Canary Yellow, 918 Orange, and 923 Scarlet Lake

Ink: Tsukineko—VersaFine Onyx Black and VersaColor Canary

Computer and color printer

Font: Doggie Bag script

Sewing machine and pink thread

½" circle punch

Paper flower: Savvy Stamps

3" length of ¼"-wide chartreuse grosgrain ribbon

Scalloped oval punch: Marvy

Sunburst punch: Punch Bunch (optional) or hand cut the sunburst

Sponge or sponge dauber

HOW TO:
Stamp the flower patch twice with black ink onto Eggshell cardstock. Color in one complete image with colored pencils and color in a single flower on the remaining image. Sponge Canary ink around the main image and over the single flower. Punch a scalloped oval out of Holly Berry cardstock and trim to size. Stitch close to the edge of the Holly Berry paper to create a border and mount the piece around the main flower patch image. Sandwich ribbon between layered strips of patterned paper and stitch together. Punch the single flower image from cardstock using the ½" circle punch. Hand cut or punch a sunburst from Key Lime cardstock. Mount all layers onto the note card. Print the word "greetings" onto paper and trim to size. Glue the "greetings" message and paper flower to the card.

Page 66 Blooming Poinsettia
MATERIALS
Stamp: Memory Box–E717 Elegant Poinsettia

White cardstock

Note card: Memory Box–Cranberry

Colored pencils: Prismacolor–937 Tuscan Red, 924 Crimson Red, 926 Carmine Red, and 916 Canary Yellow

Ink: Tsukineko–VersaFine Onyx Black and VersaMagic Thatched Straw

Yellow glitter glue

Sponge or sponge dauber

HOW TO:
Stamp the poinsettia image with black ink onto white cardstock. Color with pencils, blending from the center to the tips of the petals. Trim the cardstock ⅛" smaller than the card all around. Sponge the edges with Thatched Straw ink, rubbing the color onto the edge of the paper a little at a time until the color is deep enough. Color the center of the flower with the Canary Yellow pencil and embellish with glitter glue. Mount the image to the card.

Page 67 Snowman in a Christmas Scarf
MATERIALS
Stamps: Memory Box–D507 Mitten Snowman; Rubber Soul–1768G Season's Greetings

Cardstock: White; Memory Box–Crimson and Key Lime

Patterned paper: Memory Box–6" x 6" Christmas Brights Collection

Colored pencils: Prismacolor–(buttons) 923 Scarlet Lake; (snowman body) 1024 Blue Slate and 1087 Powder Blue; (mittens) 913 Spring Green and 989 Chartreuse

Ink: Tsukineko–VersaFine Onyx Black, VersaColor Pinecone, and VersaMagic Key Lime

Sewing machine and red thread

½" and ¼" circle punches

8" length of ⅜"-wide striped grosgrain ribbon

Sponge or sponge dauber

HOW TO:
Stamp the snowman with black ink onto white cardstock and color with pencils. Cut out a scarf shape from patterned paper and fringe the end with scissors. Glue the scarf onto the snowman. Stamp "Season's Greetings" in Pinecone ink under the scarf. Cut the paper into a tag shape and sew along the edges. Sponge the edges with Key Lime. Mount the tag onto Crimson cardstock and trim a scant ⅛" from the edges of the white cardstock. Punch a ½" circle from the Key Lime cardstock and mount at the pointed end of the tag. Punch a ¼" hole in the center of the ½" circle. Insert the ribbon through the hole and tie.

Page 68 Lacy Outline Flowers
MATERIALS
Stamps: Memory Box–F703 Open Poppy and D698 Swish Flower

Note cards: Memory Box–Water and Forget Me Not

Ink: Tsukineko–VersaMark Clear and VersaMagic Sea Breeze; Impress–Fresh Ink Freesia

White embossing powder

Sponge dauber

HOW TO:
Stamp the Open Poppy in clear ink onto the Water note card and stamp the Swish Flower in clear ink onto the Forget Me Not note card. Emboss with white embossing powder. Sponge the flowers with the dark colors first, followed by lighter colors. Use the lighter colors to rub into the darker areas to blend together.

Page 69 Confetti Shaker
MATERIALS
Stamps: Memory Box–B609 Baby Shower and B616 Solid Onesie

Hot press watercolor paper

White note card

Transparency

Watercolor markers: Marvy Le Plume II–53 Pale Blue, 99 Periwinkle, and 100 Sapphire

Ink: Tsukineko–StazOn Midnight Blue

Sewing machine and white thread

Flower confetti

Watercolor paintbrush

Foam mounting squares

HOW TO:
Color directly onto the onesie rubber stamp with all three shades of watercolor markers. Stamp the image onto the watercolor paper, and then wet the image with a paintbrush to blend the colors. Let dry and trim to size. Place a few loose pieces of confetti onto the image and layer a piece of transparency, cut slightly smaller than the watercolor paper, over the image. Stitch close to the edges. Stamp "baby shower" with Midnight Blue ink onto the transparency and let dry completely. Mount onto the white note card with foam mounting squares.

Page 69 Over the Moon
MATERIALS
Stamp: Hero Arts–B3836 Over the Moon

Note card: Memory Box–Water

Colored pencils: Prismacolor–938 White (body and stars), 993 Hot Pink (nose and udder), 916 Canary Yellow (moon), 1100 China Blue (sky), and 943 Burnt Ochre (tail)

Ink: Tsukineko–Brilliance Graphite Black

6" length of ⅜"-wide white-and-black polka-dot ribbon

Vellum tag, 1¾" diameter

HOW TO:
Stamp the cow image onto the vellum tag with black ink and let dry. Color the back of the image with colored pencils. Tie the ribbon onto the tag and mount to the card.

Page 70 A Handful of Lupines
MATERIALS
Stamp: Hero Arts–H3782 Lupine

Note card: Memory Box–Endive

Watercolor paints: Twinkling H2Os–(flowers) Royal Orchid, Bougainvillea, Pink Azalea, and Ocean Wave; (stems) Lemon Grass and Moss Green

Gold metallic thread

Transparency

Extra-fine-mist spritzer bottle (filled with water): JudiKins

HOW TO:
Paint directly onto the rubber stamp and allow the colors to dry. Mist the stamp with water to reactivate the colors and press onto the transparency. Mist the stamp again and press again, which will yield a lighter image. Reapply the paint colors as necessary. When stamping, hold the image as steady as possible so that the image doesn't slide when it touches the transparency. Repeat the process on the Endive note card. Fold the transparency around the note card so the images nearly align, and trim to size. Tie the two cards together with metallic thread around the folds.

Page 70 Three Vases

MATERIALS
Stamp: Memory Box—D421 3 Vases with Flowers

Cardstock:

Memory Box—Endive

Transparency

Self-stick notes

White acrylic paint

Watercolor paints: Twinkling H2Os—Blue Ice, Majestic Blue, Lemon Grass, and French Lilac

Ink: Tsukineko—Brilliance Graphite Black

HOW TO:
Fold the transparency in half and trim to the desired size. Unfold and lay flat. Use self-stick notes to create a rectangular box on the front of the transparency. Paint the inside of the "box" with white acrylic paint and let dry. This will be the surface to which you'll add your watercolor paints. Remove the self-stick notes and paint the white area with the watercolor paints, slightly overlapping colors and allowing them to run together. Stamp the vase image with black ink. Let dry completely. Fold the Endive cardstock in half and trim to match the transparency. Fold the transparency around the Endive card.

Page 71 Contemporary Shower Invitation

MATERIALS
Stamps: Rubber Soul—1535F Gingko Leaf and 765F Shower; Savvy Stamps—865F Ornate Pattern Background

Cardstock: White; Memory Box—Sugar Plum

Note card: Memory Box—Pink

Ink: Tsukineko—VersaMark Clear and VersaMagic Red Brick

Watercolor brush

Chalk palette (pink and light brown shades)

HOW TO:
Stamp the patterned background image with clear ink onto white cardstock. Load a dry brush with powder from a chalk palette and brush over the image to fill, using several pink and light brown shades. Stamp the Gingko Leaf with Red Brick over the patterned background. Cut the background image into two squares and one rectangle and layer onto the Sugar Plum cardstock. Trim 1/16" from the edges of the patterned pieces. Mount the layered images onto the note card and stamp "shower" in Red Brick.

Page 71 Party Lanterns

MATERIALS
Stamps: Impress—2087C Flower Lantern and 2086C Wide Lantern

Cardstock: Memory Box—Eggshell

Ink: Tsukineko—VersaMark Clear

Chalk palette (pink and orange shades)

Watercolor brush

Computer and color printer

Font: Gasoline Alley

HOW TO:
Print the invitation onto Eggshell cardstock, taking into account the horizontal orientation of the card. Fold the cardstock in half with the text on the front, and trim to size. Stamp the lanterns below the text with clear ink. Rub the dry watercolor brush onto the chalk palette, picking up powder, and then gently rub onto the lantern images in small, swirling strokes. Repeat until the images are filled in. Use a variety of pinks and oranges to create a blended image.

Page 72 Thanks for Your Friendship

MATERIALS
Stamp: Savvy Stamps—679E Floral Print

Cardstock: White; Memory Box—Sugar Plum

Note card: Memory Box—Peapod

Ink: Tsukineko—VersaMark Clear

Computer and printer

Chalk palette (pink and brown shades)

Small watercolor brush, such as a #2 round

Vellum

Sewing machine and pink thread

Font: 2Peas Rag Tag and Autumn Leaves Capone

Crescent-shaped slot punching tool and Strawberries and Cream scrapbook paint: Making Memories

HOW TO:
Stamp the floral print with clear ink onto white cardstock. Using a dry watercolor brush, apply chalk powder to the image. Use pink and brown shades and create lighter and darker areas of color. Cut four squares from the stamped paper. Mount the squares onto Sugar Plum cardstock, leaving 1/16" in between. Trim the Sugar Plum cardstock to create a 1/16" border around the stamped images. Print the greeting onto vellum and sew the vellum onto the layered papers. Tear the vellum along sewn lines. Dab scrapbook paint along the edges of the Peapod note card. Punch crescent-shaped slots into the Peapod note card and mount the layered image to the card.

Page 72 A Good Friend

MATERIALS
Stamps: Memory Box—E702 Solid Poppy; Hero Arts—F3776 Listening

Note card: White

Ink: Tsukineko—VersaMark Clear and Brilliance Pearlescent Poppy

Paper flowers: Savvy Stamps

Watercolor brush

Chalk palette (yellow and orange shades)

HOW TO:
Stamp poppy images onto the white note card with clear ink. Using a dry watercolor brush, apply chalk powder to the poppies in shades of yellow and orange. Stamp "thanks for listening" over the poppies with Pearlescent Poppy ink. Glue the paper flowers onto the note card.

RESOURCES

7 Gypsies
www.sevengypsies.com
Metal tags and embellishments

Bazzill Basics Paper, Inc.
www.bazzillbasics.com
Paper

Bellevue Art and Frame
www.bellevueartandframe.com
Watercolor pencils, paper, and water-color brushes

Hero Arts Rubber Stamps, Inc.
www.heroarts.com
Rubber stamps

Impress Rubber Stamps
www.impressrubberstamps.com
Paper, rubber stamps, inkpads, font CDs, embellishments, and shrink plastic

Li'l Davis Designs
www.lildavisdesigns.com
Embellishments

Lockhart Stamp Company
www.lockhartstampcompany.com
Rubber stamps

Making Memories
www.makingmemories.com
Paint and embellishments

Memory Box, Inc.
www.memoryboxco.com
Paper and rubber stamps

The Punch Bunch
www.thepunchbunch.com
Paper punches

Rubbermoon Stamp Company
www.rubbermoon.com
Rubber stamps

Rubber Soul
www.rubbersoul.com
Paper, rubber stamps, inkpads, and embellishments

Savvy Stamps
www.savvystamps.com
Rubber stamps and paper flowers

Tsukineko, Inc.
www.tsukineko.com
Inkpads and daubers

ABOUT THE author

Dave Brethauer has been designing cards and paper for 12 years. He and his wife, Monica, own Memory Box, Inc., a scrapbook and rubber stamp company that sells to stores all around the world. He previously wrote *Stamp in Color: Techniques for Enhancing Your Artwork* (Martingale & Company, 2000), and has taught hundreds of classes on painting and colored-pencil techniques.